t 4-50
ga
4/48

THANKS FOR YOUR TRUST

Memories of an Untamed Accountant

Harvey S. Wineberg

02 01 00 99 98 5 4 3 2 1
Library of Congress Catalog Card Number: 98-70365
International Standard Book Number: 1-56625-103-6

Cover and interior design by
Augustine Janairo Antenorcruz

Bonus Books, Inc.
160 East Illinois Street
Chicago, Illinois 60611

Printed in the
United States of America

To my wife Ellen
and my daughters,
Susan, Julie, Margi and Nancy.

They, more than anyone or anything,
have made my life more rich and full
than I could ever have imagined.

Table of Contents

ACKNOWLEDGMENTS

I owe special thanks to David Whitaker, a Chicago-based freelance writer, for his untiring help in putting this book together. I also wish to thank my friend, Elaine Weiss, past Regional Director of the U.S. Department of Health and Human Services and now Associate Executive Director of the American Bar Association. Elaine not only provided proof-reading help, but offered valuable suggestions along the way.

Finally, thanks to my wife, Ellen, for, among many things, unknowingly coming up with the main title for this book.

PREFACE

In my more than 40-year career as an accountant and financial advisor, I've had the opportunity to work with some of the most wonderful and talented people imaginable.

Some of those people have been famous sports figures; Chicago Cubs manager Leo Durocher, hockey great Bobby Hull, and Bulls sharpshooters John Mengelt and John Paxson. Others have included powerful attorneys, business leaders, medical professionals and musicians such as MCI founder John Goeken; many of the senior partners of the Sonnenschein law firm; Allan Muchin, Chairman of the law firm of Katten, Muchin, & Zavis; Ed Minor, Chairman of Robinson Steel Company; world-renowned neurosurgeon Dr. Leonard J. Cerullo; Jerry Reinsdorf, Chairman of the Chicago Bulls and Chicago White Sox; Richard Phelan, attorney and former Cook County Board President; and jazz legend Ramsey Lewis. Many other wonderful clients have not been that famous. All of them, however, by putting their financial affairs in my hands, have shown faith and trust in me over the years. For that, I am most grateful.

This book began as a simple act of expressing that gratitude. In putting my reflections on paper, however, it has evolved into a memoir of sorts. Building relationships and taking time to learn from others have, perhaps more than anything else, served as the keys to whatever success I may have had. In this book, I share those relationships and recount both personal and professional experiences that have proven invaluable to me. I also reflect on business strategies and philosophies that I hope will help others who make a career in the world of public accounting.

Though I have taken time to record my professional history to date, I have no immediate plans to retire. I am very healthy and hope and expect to work a long time, certainly as long as I feel productive.

Practicing a profession that I love has truly been one of the most rewarding aspects of my life. What a tremendous gift to have a profession that lets me provide personal and financial counsel to clients — who have become friends.

Harvey S. Wineberg

FOREWORD

Before introducing Harvey, I suppose I should introduce myself. I moved from Philadelphia to Chicago in 1970 to study with one of the foremost neurosurgeons at the time, Dr. Paul Bucy. Although my need for financial management or planning was nonexistent at the time, there were still tax forms to fill out. Accordingly, my insurance agent cum tax preparer back East referred me to a person I later discovered he did not personally know. Needless to say, I did not know him either but had the effrontery to call Mr. Wineberg around tax time to seek his help.

Naive may be an understatement when describing my understanding of Chicago business and finance at the time, and that was probably good. For whatever reason, possibly amusement, Harvey decided to take my case. The rest, as they say, is history. Our friendship grew as rapidly as my practice.

At first glance, we couldn't be more different. Harvey is tall, debonair, and svelte. He is an avid sports fan and athlete. He was born, raised, and educated in the Midwest with its inherent mores and values. He eats fast and little, and drinks less. He is card-carrying Jewish. He is a force in the field of accounting and finance, and for years has been regarded as one of the city's special people. On closer inspection, however, there are certain similarities which surface. Harvey is intensely family-oriented — "you are only as happy as your least happy child." The following pages will give ample testimony that his friendships run deep, long, and strong. He is loyal in his business relationships and in his personal relationships. Most of all, he is a wealth of aphorisms, homilies, and short (rarely funny) jokes. Does this make me a Harvey wannabe, or is Harvey the "Everyman" in all of us?

Even within the man himself, there are certain apparent paradoxes — or maybe there is just a wider spectrum of humanism. Certainly, there is the strong masculine side — the lover of baseball and basketball, the player of tennis and golf. The guru of the board room, the raconteur at dinner, the honest trustee. As the stories in this book unfold, an appreciation of the "man's man" will emerge.

On the other hand, there is the softer side. In addition to loving being putty in the hands of his wife, four daughters and grandchildren, there is Harvey the shoulder and the ear. Few of his friends have not had the opportunity to access both. Harvey will give up tickets to a Chicago Bulls game, postpone personal engagements, or even cancel a board meeting to counsel a friend in need. If Ellen Wineberg is the archetypal mother figure, Harvey is certainly the wise father/grandfather/brother. When I asked whether he would rather be portrayed as Scrooge or Marley, he answered,

"Which do you want?"

All said, I guess we're just one big family because for Harvey, friends are family and family are, above all, friends.

I am honored to have been asked to write this brief foreword to what promises to be a great read about a great man.

Leonard J. Cerullo, M.D.

CHAPTER I
The Hull Story

Although I may have fantasized about it as a kid, I certainly never really imagined my name splashed across a newspaper headline. After all, I was not a high-profile athlete, an accomplished actor, or even a budding politician. I was a certified public accountant.

"Accountant Wineberg helped the Golden Jet to work out world's biggest sports contract," read a July 5, 1972, headline in the *Chicago Daily News*. Bobby Hull, on the other hand, was a high-profile athlete. In fact, the "Golden Jet," as he was known to hockey fans everywhere, was practically the Michael Jordan of his time. The Chicago Blackhawks' celebrated left-winger was arguably the most recognized figure in all of sports. And that's how my name wound up in large print.

I had been introduced to Bobby Hull through mutual

friends. My attorney, Barry Elman and another friend, Jim Pelts, were good friends of Bobby's. My wife, Ellen, and I were pleasantly surprised one night in 1970 when Barry and his wife, Joan, and Jim and his wife, Cathy, dropped by our apartment. Bobby Hull was with them. He was warm and funny. I quickly realized why he was thought of as one of the most charismatic people around.

At 39, I had built a fairly successful career. I had my hands into quite a few things. On top of my regular duties as an accountant, I had launched a concert ticket service in Chicago that is now well-known nationally as Ticket Master (more about that later). I had also become the financial advisor to another famous Chicago sports figure, Leo Durocher.

Known affectionately around baseball as "Leo the Lip," the wise-cracking Chicago Cubs manager had become a good friend as well as a distinguished client. The business relationship I formed with Leo — which is quite a story in itself and one which I will share in the pages ahead — helped chart a course for the rest of my career. It's partly what brought Bobby Hull to my apartment that night.

Bobby said he was aware that I represented Leo. He told me his contract with the Blackhawks was up in another year. And then he asked me to represent him.

He also said there was some urgency to his request because he was being courted by Mark McCormack's International Management Group out of Cleveland. McCormack's group represented Arnold Palmer, Jack Nicklaus and others, and to this day is arguably one of the two or three powerhouses in the business, along with David Falk and Lee Steinberg.

In any case, Bobby needed a quick answer. I, of course, was somewhat in shock. After digesting the idea that I would be helping an athlete of his stature, I said yes.

Sports contracts back then, of course, weren't what they are today. As for hockey contracts, they were in perpetuity — which meant that when a player signed the contract with an NHL team, he agreed to play for so many years at so many dollars, but the team then retained an exclusive right to sign him at the end of the current contract. Short of a lawsuit, there was no way out of that, which meant a player was bound to his team for life and only the terms had to be worked out. In effect, the team held all the cards.

It was 1970 and I remember sitting at my desk at my Ticketron office in Chicago's Marina City, Bobby was with me, and McCormack's people were supposed to come in and meet with him the next day. Bobby and I signed a contract agreeing that I would represent him in all his negotiations and financial matters.

I don't remember how much my contract was for, but I know the reason Bobby came to me and didn't use McCormack was because he just couldn't abide by the fees in their proposed contracts. I believe they charged 15% for contract negotiations and then something between 25% and 35% on all endorsements and appearances. Bobby just thought that was unconscionable. Today, agent fees are pretty much regulated at 4% for contract negotiations.

In any case, Bobby wasn't able to reach them to explain he had signed with me. So when two men show up at my office the next morning expecting to meet and sign Bobby Hull, they were most surprised to learn he had just signed with me. There wouldn't be any need for a meeting.

They were more than a little upset, in fact they were quite angry. They began yelling at me, saying there's no way someone like me could represent Bobby Hull. I told them anybody

Bobby Hull wants to be represented by can represent Bobby Hull. I suggested they go represent someone who was not so important, someone who could really be helped with all of that expertise they were implying they possessed and I lacked.

I knew this was a big moment for me, the chance to represent an athlete of Bobby Hull's caliber does not come along very often — and Bobby certainly was a superstar. Even after all the smoke has cleared with the onset of other famous hockey players, a recent poll showed he is still considered the greatest left wing the game has ever seen. Gordie Howe was voted the best right winger, Wayne Gretzky the center, along with defensemen Bobby Orr and Doug Harvey and goalie Terry Sawchuck.

These men were, of course, all tough. But I never truly realized Bobby's physical power until I saw the cattle rancher in him.

During his heyday with the Hawks, Bobby's coach was Billy Reay. The team usually had Sunday night games and didn't play again until Wednesday. Because Bobby was the star, Coach Reay sometimes gave him Monday's off, and Tuesday's if a special need arose.

Besides hockey, Bobby's great love was cattle. It still is. He has a cattle herd not far from Toronto. Now, I can't tell you all of his cattle investments have been economically great, but he loved cattle, and loved taking care of them. It has been an important part of his life, and many times that's where you'd find him on his Monday's off. One Sunday in the middle of January, Bobby says to me, "Get ready. We're going up to Winnipeg on Monday, I've got a cattle sale Tuesday morning."

So I went along, and so did Pat Stapleton, a long-time Blackhawk player and captain, and a terrific person as well.

The three of us flew up to Winnipeg in a private plane. Of all the major Canadian cities, Winnipeg's landscape and climate is the worst. It's flat, and there's nothing to stop the winds, which makes it one of the coldest places you can find.

Anyway, we get out of the plane and into a waiting car. Pat and I get in the back and Bobby sits up front with the driver. I dressed as warmly as I could — sweater, coat, hat, gloves — but it wouldn't be enough. Bobby, on the other hand, is sitting in the front seat with a polo shirt open at the neck and an unbuttoned cardigan sweater.

We drive out to the auction site. It's Monday night and the auction doesn't begin until the next morning, but Bobby wants to see the animals. We come to a stop and Bobby tells us we have to walk two blocks from here. It's freezing. Stapleton grabs my arm and says, "Harvey, if you get out of this car, I'll kill you. I don't know how, and I don't know when, but I'll kill you."

We wouldn't budge. We slumped in the back of the car, just hoping to survive while Bobby begins walking with practically nothing on in what's got to be minus 70 degree wind chill. But that was Bobby, tough as superman.

I remember going with Bobby to his farm in the summertime. He'd grab the feed bags and hoist them into the air like a sack of garbage. I couldn't even move the bags, let alone pick one up. But Bobby's toughness may have rubbed off on me, at least when it came to dealing with the business side of his sport.

I remember being asked to a meeting by Alan Eagleson, who was for years the head of the Hockey Players' Association. Bobby was in the final season of his contract, he was getting his share of endorsements and commercials, and contract talks were still down the road. Ironically, the meeting was held in the bar of Chicago's Bismarck Hotel — which was owned by the Wirtz family. The Wirtz family, of course, also owned the Blackhawks, and still do. As Eagleson and I sat having a drink, he tried to convince me that Bobby Hull would be better off if he represented Bobby in contract negotiations, while I just handled Bobby's financial matters.

I firmly told him that's not what Bobby wants, and it's not what I want. I knew Bobby had already seen through Eagleson. You see, Eagleson never had any concerns about conflicts of interest. At the time, Eagleson was probably as close to the Wirtz family and other owners as he was to the players. Bobby's not only a tough guy, but a smart one. It was clear to Bobby that Eagleson was not as much a friend of the players as others thought he was. He was right.

I recently finished reading a book by Russ Conway about Eagleson's legal travails. At the time of this writing, Eagleson is charged with fraud and embezzlement. According to reports from the Toronto Sun, he agreed to a plea-bargain resulting in an 18-month jail term in Canada, revocation of his law license, and close to a million dollar fine in the U.S. He was also kicked out of the National Hockey League's Hall of Fame. Long before Eagleson's more public troubles, Bobby would have nothing to do with him, but I had thought I should at least hear what he had to say.

You could say our discussion at the Bismarck that day was a bit spirited, but tensions were eased when, much to our surprise, Charlie Finley walked into the hotel bar. The owner of the Oakland Athletics — and the future owner of the Oakland team in the WHA — recognized Eagleson and came over and introduced himself to us. We shared a brief conversation in which he revealed he was getting ready to sell the baseball team, but complained that he had signed a 15-year lease with the City of Oakland. Now it was costing him a fortune to get out of it.

Finley looked at me and said, "You know how dumb I am?" I didn't answer, but he said he could have signed a one or two-year lease instead. "But not me," he said with a disgusted laugh, "I had to be a big shot, and now it's costing me millions."

Well, I wasn't trying to be a big shot, just hoping to represent my client as best I could. When Finley left and we were able to continue our meeting, Eagleson quickly realized he wasn't getting anywhere with me. Like I said, this client of mine was tough. In working on behalf of Bobby, I got a sense of what it must be like to play alongside him. It wasn't just his toughness, but his loyalty and determination that inspired those around him to dig deeper and push harder, to expect more of their own performance. That's how I hoped to represent him, with the same support that his teammates offered him on the ice.

Not long after my meeting with Eagleson I heard from three gentlemen who felt that the National Hockey League had become a monopoly that was unreasonably restrictive. Gary Davidson, Don Regan and Ben Hatskin — Davidson and Regan were out of California, and Hatskin out of Winnipeg — decided they would start another hockey league. It wouldn't be the first time a second league had attempted to form, but these men had some significant money behind them. They also had a game plan, one which included Bobby Hull.

Davidson, Regan and Hatskin felt if they could get Bobby Hull as the kingpin of the league, it would help put them over the top. Getting Bobby would not only give the league instant credibility, it would encourage other players — players who had no way to get out of their contracts — to consider joining their league. Getting Bobby Hull might also keep this new league around long enough for it to eventually gain entry into the NHL if it couldn't make it on its own. It's awfully hard for a second league to make it anywhere and, although I didn't necessarily think about it at the time, a merger was probably one of their long-term motivations. So, these men came to Chicago and presented their plan about the league and Bobby's potential involvement with it.

Bobby was adored and worshipped in Chicago. He loved the city and its fans. He never wanted to leave in spite of the unpleasantness he experienced with the Wirtz family over the years. One of those experiences went back to the 1968 season, when Bobby had actually sat out a month or two in an attempt to get what he thought was a fair contract. But things always had a way of working out, and in 1972 Bobby and I weren't really interested in the idea of him leaving Chicago. Still, we felt we should at least hear what the three hockey entrepreneurs had to say, that it certainly couldn't hurt us in our leverage with the Blackhawks.

By this time my business partner, Steve Lewis, had just joined me. That gave me some great support because Bobby was taking up a good portion of my time. I was trying to practice accounting and resolve this contract issue while still trying to be a good father to four young daughters. It was kind of a hectic, strenuous time, but also very exciting. On and off the ice, Hull was a celebrated personality, by far the biggest draw in hockey. That's what I had on my side as serious negotiations began.

Arthur Morse was the Blackhawks' lawyer. Arthur Wirtz was Chairman of the Board. His son, William, was Team President at the time and the team's general manager was

Tommy Ivan.

Morse was very close to Irv Kupcinet, the well-known columnist for the *Chicago Sun-Times*. I remember the first few meetings with Morse were disappointing. I would get absolutely nowhere, and the next day I would read in Kupcinet's column that Bobby Hull and his agent, Harvey Wineberg, were being unreasonable, that Hull owed it to himself to stay in Chicago.

We didn't disagree with that. We wanted to stay in Chicago. I met with Morse, and at one point with GM Tommy Ivan, and had one dinner meeting that Bill Wirtz attended at the Bismarck Hotel.

I remember telling them, "Look, if nothing else, Bobby Hull is entitled to be the highest paid hockey player in the world." They told me they were willing to deliver that, so I pointed out that being the highest paid player means we want more money than the league's rising star, Bobby Orr. They conceded that could be done. I asked how do I know that. They said Orr was probably making about $150,000. I told them I had reason to believe he was making more than $200,000. Whatever the number, I said they had a way of knowing what Orr makes, and I don't. All I'm concerned with is making sure Bobby Hull becomes the highest paid hockey player in the world with his next contract.

I chronicled the negotiations as they unfolded. The following notes came from a meeting with Arthur Morse.

■ ■ ■

May 23, 1972
PRIVATE AND CONFIDENTIAL
MEMO
RE: Meeting with Arthur Morse

I met today with Arthur Morse, representing the Wirtz family and the Chicago Blackhawks, to discuss Bobby Hull's contract.

Arthur Morse made it clear that the delay of this meeting was due to his busy schedule and was not in any way intended to reflect any lack of eagerness on behalf of the Blackhawks to reach an agreement with Bobby.

He referred continually to our three previous meetings which I remember to have been back in October 1971, one of which was held at the Wirtzes office, one at his house and one at his office. At those times I was repeatedly asked what Bobby would take and I repeatedly requested that the first offer come from the Blackhawks. When pressured at the second meeting I did tell Arthur Morse that if he needed some figure to kick off from he could start with the figure reported by the newspapers to be Bobby Orr's salary, and then add something. I made it quite clear, however, that this was not an offer on my part but rather a place for negotiations to begin, and that I really wanted more than this.

Also mentioned in 1971 was Bobby's becoming part of the Blackhawk-Wirtz family when his playing days were over, whereby he would be employed in some capacity at a figure to be determined, the total contract to run ten years. Arthur Morse suggested $50,000 per year for the non-playing status and I told him that was not satisfactory.

Bobby Hull did make the statement in the first meeting that he did not want to play if he was not able to play. I understood that statement to mean that if it was mutually agreed upon or determined by an independent third party that Bobby was no longer physically able to perform, that the non-player status would then prevail. Arthur Morse apparently feels that since Bobby should have the right to decide if he can play, the Wirtzes should also have that unilateral right and said today that at any time they felt he was not capable of playing up to his physical capacity they alone would have the right to terminate this player's contract. I felt that this was an extraordinarily impossible premise to accept and one which defies all logic of the player-management contract, and I have made that clear to Mr. Morse. To accept such a premise would obviously negate any meaning of a long-term contract.

Today, Arthur Morse said he was now authorized to make a deal, whereas before this was not the case, and he said he was prepared to accept my original offer of $1 more than Bobby Orr's contract. I, in turn, made it clear that:

1. I had never made an original offer of any kind.

2. I had absolutely no knowledge of the true contents of Bobby Orr's contract, although according to Mr. Morse at a previous meeting the Blackhawks do have such knowledge.

3. That any reference to Bobby Orr's contract was only in light of the reported million dollars over five years and should be referred to only within the framework of this memorandum's previous comments.

Arthur Morse felt that if Bobby was present we could have reached an agreement. I, in turn, replied that we were more than ready to reach an agreement back in October, but for whatever reasons have not been contacted since and, of course, other factors have now entered into the picture.

Also discussed in October was an interest bearing loan to Bobby. At that time, I suggested $200,000, which would be secured by the investment made by Bobby with the funds, but on which he would not be personally liable. At that time Arthur Morse thought he could only get $60,000, but today he stated that he could make that $100,000.

Arthur Morse asked me outright if I would accept $1 more than the Bobby Orr contract and I said I could not, since I did not know what Bobby Orr's contract was for. He said if Bobby Orr's contract turned out to be $1,000,000 for five years, would I accept $1 more. I said I would have to discuss that with Bobby Hull. He made it clear that that was not an offer and I said I understood that.

He asked if whatever salary was agreed upon, would we take it over a period of years. I said with the maximum tax rate being what it is, and with deferred compensation benefitting the employer rather than the employee, that that would not be sensible from our point of view. He said that they would, in effect, be giving Bobby an annuity, and I said we would rather have the use of the money to create our own, greater annuity.

Arthur Morse continually asked me to be sure that I was no longer working with Ticketron. There is no doubt in my mind that they would have tried to use that leverage to stop me from representing Bobby or to make a better deal with them. I assured him I was not. He asked me three times did I not office over there, and I assured him that I did not.

Arthur Morse then said he hoped I understood that there was no way an established team could meet the offer of a new league. I said I understood that, and also assured him that although I was not a brilliant negotiator like him, that I was not altogether stupid, and that it only depended on the new league existing for one day for Bobby to get what he had been offered. I reminded Arthur Morse that it was he himself who said if they can make Bobby wealthy, he should grab it. Arthur Morse then said where does that leave us, and I said I have to get back to Bobby and would then get back to them.

In summary, my feelings are that if we do not worry about compensation after playing days we can get $200,000 a year, with all the other minor provisions that we want. I would remind us both that our original feelings in the pre-WHA days were that $150,000 for three years with no fringes would be great.

Morse also asked if I was aware of the provision in Bobby's contract which obligates him to play again for the Blackhawks next year at a price to be determined. I pointed out to him that I was aware and that the new league was aware. He said any attempt by Bobby to play for the new league would be fought in court on that basis. I left him one final thought, and that was that under any circumstances we wanted a no-trade, no-cut contract without Bobby's prior approval. Morse said he thought that would be impossible and I said that I did not understand why that should be the case since they wanted to make Bobby a part of the family in any case. He said, but they just traded Willie Mays and I said, yes, but Willie Mays and Oscar Robertson both had first right of refusal on being traded.

Open points not covered in this meeting were: $145,000 deferred compensation, $92,000 loan and interest, playoff money, curved stick, Players Association and Addison home mortgage interest.

■ ■ ■

The Blackhawks never told me Bobby Orr's salary, and they never came up from their figure of about $150,000, despite the stature of Bobby Hull and despite the knowledge that a new league, the World Hockey Association, might try to lure their superstar away.

This went on for a number of months, and they just never gave Bobby any positive signals. Everybody in this world wants to be wanted, and they never gave Bobby Hull the feeling that he was wanted as a person, or as a player.

While the Blackhawks continued their sluggish approach to negotiations, I had occasional conversations with the people at the WHA. One day Bobby called me and said, "Harvey, I've just had it with these people. They just don't care about me, they never have, and they never will. I don't want to leave, but get me what you can...."

■ ■ ■

May 23, 1972
PRIVATE AND CONFIDENTIAL
MEMO
RE: Bobby Hull - WHA

This memorandum will reduce to writing the essence of my conversations in April, 1972, with both Ben Hatskin and Gary Davidson.

Discussed was a contract with the Winnipeg Jets of the World Hockey Association, whereby Bobby Hull would sign as a player or player-coach.

Financially the arrangement was a million dollar bonus for signing, one half paid upon signing and the other half paid into a U.S. bank under Bobby Hull's name, which he could receive sometime in 1972 — either once the first game had been played or, at the latest, so it can be reported on Bobby's 1972 U.S. income tax return. Also agreed upon was a four-year contract at $250,000 per year, also to be put in escrow in a bank, and to be earned by Bobby ratably as he performs as a player. Interest on these funds would accrue to the benefit of the Winnipeg team, whereas interest on the first million dollars, until paid, would accrue to Bobby.

This $2,000,000 would unconditionally be paid to Bobby immediately upon the league ceasing to exist or operate for any reason. If Bobby should not play for the World Hockey Association because they are not in operation, he would be entitled to the $2,000,000, but would also be entitled to any other earnings from hockey that may be paid to him by anyone else, including the NHL.

The above referred to contract would be for ten years. The fifth year would also be for $250,000 and the sixth to tenth year would be for $150,000 per year, as a coach or other executive, making the total $3,000,000. The last million would not be guaranteed by the WHA or Winnipeg Jets in any way.

It was understood that there is a clause in the present Chicago Blackhawk contract which, in effect, is a reserve clause requiring Bobby to re-sign with the Blackhawks. It was agreed that should the NHL try to enforce this provision all legal costs would be borne by the new league and that Bobby would be entitled to all compensation even if he were enjoined from playing for any length of time. It was also agreed that Bobby's contract as a player-coach-executive could not be assigned to any other WHA team nor can he be traded to another team without his prior written approval. It was further understood that Bobby would have a meaningful voice in the Players Association.

Finally, it was clear that the consideration for much of the above was that Bobby Hull would become a league asset and would make himself available for promotion of the league in any way possible, in conjunction with which both parties wish to meet with Bobby personally, to receive his assurance that he would, in effect, do all in his power to make sure the new league was a success. All endorsements or contracts now in force would remain Bobby's. All future endorsements, whether by way of the new league or personally, would be shared between Bobby and the new league in an equitable manner to be determined.

It was agreed that under no circumstances would the WHA do anything to hurt Bobby's present reputation or negotiations with the Blackhawks nor would Bobby do or say anything that would jeopardize the status of the new league. No press conference, however, would be held until there was $2,000,000 in cash on deposit in the proper bank.

■ ■ ■

The *Chicago Tribune*'s Bob Verdi, then and now one of the great sports writers in the country, called me the same day Bobby did. He asked me, what the hell's going on? Verdi really latched onto this story early, asking the right questions before anyone else did. I told him I'm not sure, but I think Bobby's about at the end of his rope, and we may wind up out of here. Verdi wrote an article to that effect, which really blew things out of the water.

Although the Hawks then made their last ditch effort of an offer, it was too little too late. After a few more weeks of negotiation we agreed on a contract with the WHA and the Winnipeg Jets that gave Bobby a million dollar signing bonus on behalf of the league, and a five-year contract at $250,000 a year, plus a lot of added guarantees — for example, if the league didn't make it and Bobby had to sell his house at a loss, the league would be responsible.

Years later, I read that the Blackhawks' decision to, in effect, lose Bobby Hull, cost them somewhere between $50 and $100 million in hard money — primarily in the form of increased salaries, legal fees and attendance. In their many years of managing the franchise, I know the Wirtz family considers this their biggest mistake.

Before flying to Winnipeg to introduce Bobby to the city, we landed in St. Paul, where Bobby signed the personal service agreement for $1 million. We received the check in the United States so that Canada would have no claim on that money, since their taxes were significantly higher than ours.

The NHL, of course, didn't take lightly to this attack on their manhood. They sued the WHA in federal court in Philadelphia. They sued Bobby, and they sued me. They sued everybody else that had anything to do with this whole thing. And they lost, as well they should have.

The presiding judge, Judge Leon Higginbotham, ruled that NHL contracts were unconscionable, that you could not bind a player the way the league had. The NHL was suing on the theory that Bobby had no right to sign with any other professional hockey team. With their courtroom defeat, the WHA was born.

When Bobby left Chicago for Winnipeg and the start of his new adventure, my wife, Ellen, and I had a going-away party for him at our house. We invited some friends that Bobby got to know through the years. We didn't tell anybody else because we didn't want to embarrass him or put him under any undue stress, but it wasn't long before the whole neighborhood realized Bobby Hull was at the Wineberg house.

By the time he came over, we must have had 20 to 30 kids in the house. I'm telling you he said hello to each of those children, gave each an autograph, talked to all of them and was as pleasant and charming as a person could be. When the kids eventually left, he said good-bye to each of them by name. That's a talent that I'm sure he's learned to develop over the years, but as long as I have known Bobby he has always been a genuinely caring man. I think he felt he was blessed with so much that he should go out of his way to give back to people whenever he could. He relied not just on his athletic talent, but his keen sense of humor and natural flair for storytelling to make people feel comfortable around him.

My favorite Bobby Hull story, which Bobby still tells in English or fluent French, recalls the pride of the Montreal Canadians in their heyday. After every game, Maurice "The Rocket" Richard, the Canadians' former player turned color commentator, would pick the three stars of the game. One night when the Blackhawks played the Canadians in Montreal, Richard said the trois (or number three) star of the game was Claude Provost, the best defensive forward ever to play the game. The deux (or number two) star of the game was Richard's younger brother Henri "The Pocket Rocket" Richard, who skated faster than any man on ice. The un, or number one, star of the game that evening went to the Canadians team captain, Jean Beliveau, one of the game's all-time greats. Honorable mention, Richard said, goes to Bobby Hull of the Blackhawks, who tonight had three goals and two assists. Chicago lucky to win 5–3.

Bobby eventually took that personality of his — along with a mighty slap shot — to Winnipeg, where he received a very warm welcome. Hull liked the city and his teammates. He especially liked playing with the two top players from Sweden, Ulf Nilsson and Anders Hedberg. Though he never regularly skated on the line with the Blackhawks' great Stan Mikita, Bobby did skate with a lot of good ones in Chicago. But, he told me he never felt like he meshed with anybody as well as he did with Nilsson and Hedberg. After Bobby stopped playing, the two Swedes ended up becoming stars with the NHL's New York Rangers.

Winnipeg had a very good team while Bobby was there, but it sure took some patience to get up to see him. The trek took me through Minneapolis and Grand Forks. After each game, Bobby would spend two hours signing autographs. We'd finally get something to eat about midnight and then get back to his house at about 2 a.m.

Bobby always insisted I stay at his house, but it's become pretty well-known that his house was not always the calmest of places. He and his wife, Joanne, who I always got along with really well and who I know trusted me, had their share of problems. They eventually divorced and Joanne is remarried and living in Vancouver.

Bobby just kept playing hockey. Five teams eventually merged into the NHL and the WHA disbanded. But before Bobby returned to the NHL with the Buffalo Sabres, he played for the Hartford Whalers in 1980.

Bobby always was somewhat outspoken about the ills of the hockey establishment, and although he proved time after time to be right, it probably cost him a job in hockey when his career was over. Many star players like Bobby went on to work for the league or in the front office of an NHL team. But he established his independence early on in his career, and didn't seem to mind that it left him with less of an opportunity within the sport once he retired. He moved on with life without bitterness, making personal appearances, enjoying his farming and pursuing other endeavors.

He also spent as much time as possible with his children from his marriage to Joanne, but Bobby, Jr., Blake, Brett, Bart and Michelle certainly struggled through their parents divorce. Brett, of course, has become one of the great hockey players of his day. Bobby and Blake were also outstanding hockey players, but they never made it as far. Blake is now a golf pro and Bobby, Jr. is doing some other things in the world of sports. Bart was a great baseball player from what I heard and Michelle quite a figure skater.

Bobby later married a young woman named Debbie, who is a wonderful wife to him and mother to Jessica. For a while they lived up near Toronto on their farm, but also had a home in Naples, Florida. Bobby is still extremely active, not only in the cattle world but doing a lot of endorsements, commercials, appearances and autograph sessions. Because Naples isn't the easiest place to get in and out of, a few years ago they moved back to Chicago. It's where they think they belong, and so do I.

I still handle all of Bobby's financial and tax affairs, and I hope Bobby knows what a pleasure it has been to know him — as an advisor and a friend.

He and Leo Durocher were the most exciting and well-known people with whom I've worked. The relationship I formed with each of them came at an opportune time for my practice. It was the beginning of the agency explosion in sports, which was a direct result of the salary explosion in sports.

Because of these men I was able to choose whether to hold myself out as an agent or to just pursue the financial, tax and investment aspects of accounting. Or, I could do a bit of both.

My partner Steve and I discussed this at length, and the decision was clear. We wanted what we had always wanted for our firm. We did not want to become sports agents. We wanted to be full service financial planners, advisors and accountants. We conceded, however, that some of our clients — primarily athletes — might require unique services, like contract or endorsement negotiations. It was this aspect of the business that set us apart from other firms early on, and provided us diverse, challenging and fulfilling work for years to come.

CHAPTER II
More Than An Agent

In the eyes of many, representing Bobby Hull in contract negotiations made me a sports agent. The fact that I had done the same for Leo Durocher and would eventually do it for many others, including John Paxson of the Chicago Bulls, offered more testimony to that belief. In fact, I still get calls from those who assume that's what the firm of Wineberg and Lewis, P.C., specializes in.

But the truth is, I never really considered myself a sports agent. I saw myself as a certified public accountant and financial advisor to a variety of clients. One of the duties of serving as advisor to athletes and sports celebrities was representing them in contract negotiations. But that aspect of it was never something I, or the firm, set out to specifically handle. I have no real doubt that we made the right decision in maintaining our broad range of services.

The life of an agent is not one to which I aspired for a variety of reasons. Representing an athlete in contract negotiations is fraught with the peril of that athlete leaving for another agent for no particular reason. It happens to agents all the time.

On top of that, the pursuit of a client can get pretty aggressive. There are agents and "chasers" on behalf of agents who are recruiting kids as early as grammar school. That's right, grammar school. If a kid shows extraordinary talent at a young age he is likely to have an agent or two keeping an eye on him or trying to befriend him.

Obviously there's been a history of agents offering money or other benefits to potential players, their families, even their high school or college coaches. They basically buy their clients.

Now, I'm not saying they're doing anything illegal, but that's not to say they're doing everything legal. I know someone who decided to try his hand at being an agent. He went to Kansas to meet with officials of the National Collegiate Athletic Association (NCAA) and was told if you don't start dealing with hot prospects in high school or before, you have a tough time getting them out of the clutches of the bigger agents.

When it comes to being an agent, there's no better pitch than name recognition. There's this theory that because I represent Superstar X, I can do better for you. There may be some validity to that, and certainly a successful track record is good for any business, but I don't think it's always that simple in this particular field. As I mentioned, part of this has to do with the fact that it's not always a clean game.

With a lot of media attention and a judicial crackdown on

these practices, such abuse seems to have declined. However, there will always remain a degree of hand-holding with the potential of crossing the line of proper representation, advising or whatever you want to call it.

Some of the things agents have done over the years to keep their clients happy is just something I couldn't have been a part of. Although I may have been well positioned to take that route, and although that route may have been more lucrative in the long run, it just wasn't what I wanted to do. It wasn't something that best fit my personality or my business sense.

Instead, we continued to be what we were: CPAs with a personal service practice that cared about people and their long-term needs. We did, and still do, tax work, financial planning, accounting and, in broad terms, investment advising.

The athletes who were a great part of our practice early on — maybe as much as 20% or 25% in the early 1980s — gradually diminished to the point that they are no longer a significant portion of our clientele. Part of the reason for the decline in our involvement with athletes was due to changes in the tax laws, and part was due to our conscious effort to stabilize our practice by avoiding a concentration of clients in one industry — a volatile one at that.

Before coming to that conclusion, however, a number of athletes passed through our doors. The attention that came with representing Bobby Hull, and signing him to a historic contract, certainly raised our visibility in the sports world.

Bill Melton and Ken Henderson, who both played for the Chicago White Sox and probably heard of me through Bobby, became my first baseball clients.

Melton was an all-star third baseman who led the American League in home runs in 1971. He and his wife,

Tess, remain good friends of ours and Bill again works for the White Sox. His story is an interesting one.

Bill was pretty much in the prime of his career when he fell off the roof of his house in California trying to paint or repair something, and he hurt his back pretty severely.

In those days there was an enzyme injection popular in Canada that many people considered a successful alternative to major surgery. It was apparently quite effective in treating disc problems. Although it had not yet been approved in the U.S., Dr. Lyman Smith was doing some testing of the enzyme for the FDA at a hospital in suburban Chicago. He worked on Bill's back. One of the conditions of the enzyme's regulation was that the doctor could never operate or use this injection on any one person more than one time.

Although the first injection seemed quite successful, there was apparently some need for a second treatment. So not long after this diagnosis, Bill checked back into the hospital under his mother's maiden name.

Word got out that Bill had had the second procedure done by the same doctor, and I believe the doctor's license may have been suspended for a short time.

Bill returned to the game and had a few more solid years, but he was never quite the same, never could regain full strength in his swing.

Before all of this, however, I remember getting both Melton and Henderson very good contracts with the White Sox, but it was through this work that I also got a taste of how the agent game sometimes works.

One of the first baseball agents to hit the big money was a man named Jerry Kapstein. He began his career in sports public relations. By hanging around the NBA's Baltimore Bullets' basketball camp, he eventually got enough clients to launch his own agency. He later got into representing baseball players and made quite a name for himself.

I remember having a few business-related phone conversations with him, and when I began representing Melton and Henderson he seemed to call me more often. He once told me I had done a terrific job for those two players, which, in those days probably meant I got them $90,000 or $100,000.

Anyway, Kapstein tells me he's representing the well-known ballplayer Joe Rudi, and he asks me if he could use my success figures as leverage in his negotiations. I tell him I have no problem with that. After that, when I would try to contact him, he would never return my calls. He was not one of my favorite people.

One of my favorite people, however, was the head of the baseball players association, Marvin Miller. Without a doubt Miller did more for players in all sports than anyone else in history. He paved the way for free agency and arbitration, etc., offering players the chance to shop their skills between contracts, to seek their greatest value in the marketplace. He was also of great help to me.

Whenever I had questions, he was the man to call. He was unbelievable. He would always spend all the time I needed, and when I was about to hang up he would say, "Now, are you sure you understand everything? Because I'll answer them as long as you want."

If Marvin was busy, he would always call me back as soon as he could. So, it doesn't surprise me a bit that players loved him and respected him so much, or that he had such success.

I know a lot of the owners disliked him, and they had good reason. They were overmatched. It was certainly true when I was representing Bobby that the owners in all sports had the muscle. It's also true that the pendulum has swung the other way, causing many problems — not the least of which involves big versus small markets. On the other hand, I have trouble understanding why the players shouldn't get everything that someone is willing to pay them. That's baseball's problem, in my opinion. They are unable to control their owners.

I have no way of verifying this story, but I was told that when Peter Ueberroth was commissioner of baseball he had all the owners in a room and basically said to them, all right, you have a black button and a red button in front of you. You can push the black button, and you will not win the World Series, but you will make a few dollars. You push the red button and you'll win the World Series, but lose a lot of money. Then, he supposedly said, the problem is almost all of you would push the red button. I was also told that's one of the reasons why he was not retained as commissioner.

I've always had problems understanding, for example, why Ryne Sandberg of the Chicago Cubs took a lot of heat when the Tribune paid him six million bucks in the prime of his career. I don't understand it. If the Tribune doesn't pay Ryne Sandberg, the Tribune keeps it. Now, I understand that eventually the public has to pay for some of this, but it's television that really pays for most of it. Why is it Sandberg's fault for accepting what his bosses think he's worth?

Between the television station (WGN), the attendance and everything else, the Tribune Company has to be making a fortune off the Cubs. I don't know why anyone should begrudge the players their salaries.

I recently read that all three supporting stars of the Seinfeld show are getting $600,000 a show, and Jerry Seinfeld is getting a million dollars a show. I see no problem with that. They must be worth it to those who are paying them.

On the other hand, players often learn the art of manipulation from agents. Although I'm convinced Dick Allen and Bill Madlock are both nice people, I did have a business relationship with each of them that didn't work out as well as I would have liked.

Dick Allen came to me after having had a brilliant but stormy career. I told him I'd help him, but made it clear I can't help him if he's working with anyone else at the same time. I told him that our contracts with athletes allow you to cancel on 30 days notice at any time. We're not trying to tie you up, I said, we're not interested in working with you if you're also being advised by someone else. It's just not good business.

Allen said fine, the only thing he wanted from me is to at least get him free clothes in return for endorsements. He said he'd also like to secure a book contract, "because I'd really like to write a book."

I told him he'd probably be more successful doing the free clothes deal on his own, but I did have some access to publishers. I dealt with the famous book agent Swifty Lazar when Leo Durocher wrote his biography, and had contacts with publishers as well. Sure enough, I came up with a publisher who was willing to give Dick a very good deal.

We were working on the arrangements when the publisher called me back and said, "You should know that you're not the only person out there who's negotiating a publishing deal for Dick."

That's great, I thought. I called Allen, and he immediately acknowledged the truth. He told me he had been so mistreated, as he put it, by past agents that he never believed or trusted anybody. He said that's why he was exploring all the options he could. I said that's fine, I'm sure someone else can take care of you, because I won't. I got an autographed picture from him, and that's about it.

The Bill Madlock situation wasn't much different. For months we were strung along by Madlock and Steve Greenberg. Steve is the son of Hall of Famer Hank Greenberg, and he and Madlock were close friends. Steve was also a lawyer and ultimately, I think, talked Madlock into having him handle everything himself.

Everyone certainly has the privilege of choice, but there comes a time when honesty cannot only be a great equalizer, but it can save a lot of time.

Perhaps that element of evasiveness will always be a part of negotiating. It seems to me, however, that there are more effective ways of not showing your hand.

Obviously, my experience with the Blackhawks during the Hull negotiations was a bit slippery. I had no way of knowing what Bobby Orr made at the time, and the Blackhawks were willing to take advantage of that.

Ironically, I had a similar experience with the Blackhawks after the Hull negotiations. I had no idea how accurate a foreshadowing that experience would be.

I agreed to represent a player named J.P. Bordelau. I remember walking into the office of Blackhawks' General Manager Bob Pulford one day, at his request, to talk about Bordelau's contract. Pulford was sitting at his desk and didn't seem to notice me. I stood for a few minutes. He didn't move and didn't say a word.

I finally said good morning, and still got no response. He eventually acknowledged my presence and, as you might have guessed, we had a very unsatisfactory negotiation.

Pulford tried to convince me Bordelau was the fourth highest paid player on the Blackhawks, and that that was much higher than he should be. I knew a lot of Blackhawks players and their salaries, and I knew Bordelau wasn't one of the top four. This tug-o-war continued for several weeks, but despite Pulford's resistance we eventually signed a solid contract.

As an aside, I taught a semester at Columbia College in Chicago, a course entitled, "The Business of Professional Sports and Entertainment." During my time there the Blackhawks held "Banner Night" at the old Chicago Stadium and I happened to be at the game that night. One of the signs read, in big bold letters, "Will Rogers never met Bob Pulford." The next day in class one of my students asked me if I was at the game the previous night. I told him I was, and he said that was his banner. I said, "Prove it and you get an 'A' in the course." Through witnesses, he did prove it, and he did get an 'A' (he would have gotten an 'A' anyway). And that's how I felt about Bob Pulford.

Later, when Hull was still with the team but considering offers from the WHA, I wound up representing two other Blackhawks. Gerry Pinder, a forward, and Paul Shmyr, a defenseman. They were both starters and good hockey players. They were also the type of players the new league was interested in. They were relatively young and well-known, without being superstars who were going to break the bank.

Some time early on in our involvement with Hull, the two of them asked if we would represent them. We did and they both moved over to the WHA. Ironically, Gerry's brother Herb became a business associate of ours.

Herb was quite a hockey player himself and was said to be of major league caliber. But when he hurt his knee playing junior hockey, he concentrated on his education. He graduated from Harvard University Business School and Harvard Law School. After getting his degrees, he moved back to Saskatoon. The Pinder family owned a major drugstore chain in Saskatoon and Regina.

When Herb returned home, one of his many endeavors included becoming a sports agent, primarily representing hockey players. He came to know us through Gerry and thought it would be a great association if he represented the Canadian hockey players on their contracts, while we represented them for all financial and tax matters. We agreed.

We had a long and healthy relationship with Herb and his people. In 1986, however, I told my partner Steve that I could see the beginning of the end of that relationship. It was nothing personal, and Herb Pinder eventually decided to get into the financial management part of the business himself.

The end of that relationship was actually spurred by a change in the tax laws. The 1986 Tax Reform Act, in effect, was greatly designed to alter the way real estate ventures worked in the United States. All the players we represented were U.S. players, if not U.S. citizens, and, therefore, had to file U.S. returns. Up until 1986 the depreciation and other deductions, in effect, enabled a player to, for instance, put $25,000 into a real estate venture, save at least $25,000 in taxes and then at some later date sell the property at what was, hopefully, a significant gain on which he would pay a low capital gains tax.

That strategy worked well in the late 1970s and the first half of the 1980s. Remember, at the time athletes weren't making big money — even the great ones like Bobby Hull — but they were making enough to live comfortably. So we took some of the money that would have gone to the government and put it into these ventures. We never got paid anything extra for the investment advice. As an act of good faith, I often invested right along with them.

We didn't go into deep tax shelters, no three-to-one or six-to-one write-offs. Ours were almost always two-to-one write-offs, but a two-to-one write-off at a 50% tax rate, which it was in those days, meant that you could write off twice what you put in and save the 50%.

We didn't do it only for tax reasons, but for economic reasons as well. Most of them worked out well for our people. The ones that didn't work out so well were to some extent due to the real estate recession in the late 1980s and early 1990s. But even with those, we found that if you pushed the pencil, the write-offs were so great at a high rate and the recapture was at low rates, that the taxpayer still usually came out ahead.

Anyway, that was our motivation, that at worst you would come out a little ahead, and at best you would do very well. That worked fine until they changed the law disallowing those kinds of write-offs against ordinary income.

Still, there were financial rewards for our practice in the early days of the WHA. I remember when Paul Shmyr and Gerry Pinder and a few other players we represented were all with the WHA's Cleveland hockey team. When I traveled to Cleveland to meet with the owners, it was obvious who had the leverage. It was a nice feeling walking into a meeting and saying, okay, what do you want to do about these six fellows? These guys were the heart of the team, too. Again, the money wasn't huge, but our clients were happy with the job we did for them.

Representing players like these also presented unique opportunities that didn't involve a financial reward. In 1974, we chose to join the WHA all-star team on a trip to Russia and Czechoslovakia. Two years before that, Alan Eagleson had arranged for a series between the Canadian Hockey All-Stars and the Russian Hockey All-Stars in Moscow. The WHA decided to launch a similar trip. This was back when there was still a lot of political tension between the East and the West, not to mention the fierce hockey rivalry that existed between the regions. It promised to be an incredible experience for everyone.

Bobby Hull agreed to play for the WHA Canadian All-Stars along with Gordie Howe, Paul Shmyr and Frank Mahovlich, among others, and Coach Billy Harris. Because I represented Bobby and Paul, Ellen and I decided to make the trip as well.

Paul Shmyr's wife, Shirley, also went. She and Ellen got along famously. The team actually went over a week before we did. They stopped in Sweden, Finland and Norway to play a few games before getting to Russia. We met them in Russia then joined them for a game in Prague before heading back home.

In 1974, the Cold War was at its height, which certainly made things interesting. It took us a long time to clear customs in Russia. They double-checked our visas, and seemed to be looking for trouble. But the sting of the Cold War hit the players while they were trying to rest up for the game. Not only were their rooms conveniently overlooking a noisy construction site, they also received prank phone calls until four in the morning.

At this hotel, "The Russia," every floor had its own security person — in our case a woman. You gave her your key when you left the hotel, and then you got it back from her when you returned. I got the feeling they went through our rooms pretty carefully while we were gone.

Frank Mahovlich and his wife had been there before in 1972 and had a particular paranoia about all of this — they were convinced they had been followed on their last trip and that their phones were tapped — so this time they were going to be sure to examine their room. After dissecting the phone and searching the room, they began feeling under the carpet. Underneath the carpet they found a large cylindrical disk that they were sure was some type of recording mechanism. They carefully unscrewed the disc... and the chandelier in the room below them fell to the floor! Although I heard that story secondhand, I do believe it's true.

I don't think it was a terribly pleasant trip for the Mahovlich's, but because we didn't let our suspicions run wild, we had an exciting time. On the way back, we stopped in Prague for a day and there was a tour organized for the women who wanted to look at crystal and lace. The men went on a separate sight-seeing bus tour of Prague. I was the only non-hockey player on the bus — with the exception of a very good-looking Czech guide named Danielle — and I sat toward the back just looking out as the city went by. Danielle was about 28 years old at the time. At one point in the trip she sat down next to me and asked who all of these people were. I told her these were the most famous hockey players in the world, that she should meet them. I told her I was the only one here who wasn't very well-known. She said, "I don't want to be with them, I want to be with you."

She sat with me through the whole tour and, along the way, I learned she was divorced and had a young daughter. As we were leaving she asked where I was going. I told her I was going back to my hotel. She said why don't you come with me? I told her, well, I guess there's three reasons. First, I'm really not sure about the politics in this country, and, secondly, there's a dinner I have to be at tonight. Third, and most importantly, my wife is waiting for me.

When I got back to the hotel room I told Ellen this beautiful, young lady was after her husband. She said, yeah, right, you're just like all the guys who fly and think all the flight attendants are after them. I'm just telling you what happened, I exclaimed. Ellen remained skeptical.

Sure enough, the next day we're at the airport getting ready to leave and there's Danielle about 50 yards away yelling, "Good-bye, Harvey. Have a good trip." Ellen finally believed me.

A year or so later, Bill Gofen, a friend of mine who runs a very successful investment money management firm in Chicago, joined us for dinner one night and at one point he said, "By the way, Danielle said to say hello to you." What? Bill tells me he was recently in Prague on business and met this lady tour guide named Danielle. Bill said she asked where he was from, and when he said Chicago she immediately asked, "Do you know Harvey Wineberg?" He was duly impressed.

I've never gotten back to Prague and have never seen Danielle again. Obviously, I will forever be flattered by her friendliness. I hope she's doing well.

When we got on the plane in Prague that day — it was an Air Canada flight — the flight attendant welcomed everyone and then, as usual, began letting us know what refreshments were available and the cost of drinks.

I think it was Paul Shmyr who led the insurrection, but he was quickly joined by many others when they protested the drink charge. Here they had just traveled all the way to Russia to defend their hockey homeland, and they were being charged to have a beer on their way back. That was the argument, and it didn't last long. The flight attendant quickly saw the wisdom of offering drinks on the house, which made for a lively end to a truly exciting trip.

That reminds me of another one of hockey's interesting

people, Orest Kindrachuck, who we still represent. He now works for Equitable in New Jersey, but Kindrachuck was one of the "Broad Street Bullies" of the great Philadelphia Flyers' teams of the 1970s. He played alongside men like Bobby Clarke, Bernie Parent and Reggie Leach. The players' wives have a charitable organization called Flyers' Wives Fight For Lives. They had an event every year, and part of that event one year was an auction that included merchandise like Bobby Clarke's jersey and Bernie Parent's goalie stick.

Apparently Clarke's jersey raised a lot of money, but for some reason Bernie Parent's stick was not a hot item. Maybe it was because the night before, in a game against Buffalo, Parent gave up six goals in a scoring fest that ended in a tie.

The bid was stuck at $400 when Kindrachuck went up to the podium, grabbed the microphone and said, "You people don't seem to understand. This is a very valuable stick. This is the same stick Bernie used last night in our game against Buffalo. There's not a mark on it." Well, that went over big, and the stick ended up selling for about $1,200.

Kindrachuck was just one of a number of hockey players we represented besides Bobby Hull. Some of them included: Gary Jarrett, Ron Ward, Ernie Wakely, Brad McCrimmon, Ryan Walter, Blair Chapman, Alan Kerr, Trent Yawney, Rick Wamsley, Joe Daley, Bill Hajt, Mike Rogers, J.P. Bordelau, Dave Parro, Darrin Veetch, Billy Watson, Peter McNab, David Richter, Curt Giles, Glen Hanlon and Brent Ashton.

We still do tax work for many of them, but most have long since stopped playing and are now living in Canada. These men are terrific people, and we were fortunate to get to know them.

Several years ago two of the best known Blackhawks asked us to do their financial work, but insisted we keep alive corporations they had formed which allowed them double pension deductions (their own and the NHL's). We refused and, as a result, never did work with them. Years later a number of hockey and basketball players were heavily fined and penalized for doing just that. A few even had to declare bankruptcy.

We are often faced with these kinds of decisions. Assuming there is nothing illegal, my litmus test has always been to determine whose side I would rather argue in court.

Although I like hockey (it could do without the fighting) and am lucky enough to have gotten to know some of the game's greatest players, my favorite sport has always been basketball. I played a lot of it as a kid, but have concentrated more on tennis as I've gotten older. Still, my greatest excitement when working with athletes has come from working with basketball players — probably because it was this game that I always admired most.

The publicity surrounding the Bobby Hull contract pushed my name into a lot of sports circles, including that of basketball great Jack Marin. Marin had made quite a name for himself in college. At 6 feet 7 inches, he was an All-American, left-handed forward at Duke University. He was drafted fifth overall and joined the Baltimore Bullets of the NBA in 1966. He was paid $18,500 (the third highest rookie salary).

Eventually, Marin was traded to Chicago and felt he was in need of representation. The father of Marin's roommate in college had read about me and my work with Bobby Hull. He's the one who suggested Jack give me a call.

I remember meeting Jack at the Evanston Golf Course, where we talked a little bit before he teed off. Like a lot of athletes, Jack was and is a terrific golfer. He is still one of the stars on the celebrity golf tour.

We hit it off well that day, but I remember Jack telling me he didn't need to pay someone to handle his bills. He reminded me he was a mature adult with a solid education behind him.

I told him that was fine, that we'd do whatever he'd like us to do. That's our approach with everybody. He said why don't you just handle my taxes and investments, and I'll worry about my bills and things like that. Fine.

It was a couple of months later when he called and said he'd decided it's not any great sign of maturity to be able to pay bills, so we started handling all of his financial work and did so for many years. We also became great friends.

Jack was a real car aficionado. He always had three or four cars at a time, but he'd have to rebuild the front seats into the back so he could fit into them. He used to come to our house on weekends and take my kids out for rides. God knows how fast he was going. When the kids see him now, they remember how much they loved it when he'd come by — they especially remember those speed rides.

We handled Jack's contract with the Bulls in 1976. He became the Bulls starting forward and played very well for several seasons. Toward the end of his career he suffered a nagging injury and told me he wasn't sure if he should play one more year or go back to law school.

I told him I'd make an appointment with Jonathan Kovler, who was the Bulls' general manager at the time, to see what their interest was. Then Jack could decide from there.

Before the appointment, Jack called me and said he would like to go with me. I told him no, that although Kovler was a decent person, he wasn't always the easiest to negotiate with. I said they're going to cut your salary by 50% and you're going to swear at them and then get up and walk out of the room. I don't need you there to do that. Jack says, no, I promise. "I just want to sit there and listen because some day I think I want to be an agent, and I just want to learn."

So Jack walked in with me. We sat down, talked to Kovler for a couple minutes and, sure enough, Kovler says we think we should cut you 60%. Jack swore at him, got up and walked out of the room.

We eventually reached some agreement, but the Bulls refused to guarantee it, which, considering how long Jack had been in the league and how well he played, didn't make much sense to us. So Jack left the game, took the LSAT test and got one of the highest grades in the country and graduated from Duke University Law School. Since then he's been practicing law in Durham, North Carolina, where he and his wife, Robin, who has her own successful catering business, have raised their son John.

Before Jack finally left the Bulls, however, he gave me an autographed team picture. But in this picture, Jack has his back turned to the camera, his name and number clearly visible on the back of his jersey. He autographed it this way: "To Harvey, Thank you for making it possible for me to turn my back on the NBA."

Jack now also serves as an agent, representing Vinnie Del Negro of the San Antonio Spurs among others. Through Jack, we handle the financial aspects of Vinnie's affairs. Vinnie's a fabulous person and a great ball player. For two years he played for Benneton Treviso in Italy's professional league. He was one of only two non-Italians. The Bulls' Tony Kukoc was the other.

When Vinnie was in Chicago a couple years ago, we played golf and had dinner. Not only did Vinnie's wife and mother-in-law join us, but also Tony Kukoc, his wife and his incredibly mature two-year-old son. My partner, Steve Lewis, is as close to Vinnie as I am to John Paxson.

Marin introduced us to other players as well, including John Mengelt and Tate Armstrong. We also met with Jerry Sloan, the former Bulls' great and current coach of the Utah Jazz .

Our work with Jerry was brief, but interesting. At the time, he was looking for an advisor on wills and estate planning. He was in search of contrarian advice, because he said he really didn't want to leave anything to his children or to charity.

His rationale was that when he and his brothers and sisters were growing up, the only thing his parents gave them was food and basic clothing. They had to work for anything else they needed or wanted. He told me he had a paper route from as early as he can remember. He felt that was the best thing that anyone had ever done for him. He didn't want to pay taxes on his estate, and he didn't want to leave it to charity. I don't know what he ended up doing, but I believe he eventually worked with a neighbor of his on this issue, maybe putting the money in some long-term trusts.

Although unusual, I thought this philosophy was indicative of Sloan's strong moral fiber. At ten years, he now has the longest tenure with the same team of any coach in the NBA. He coaches the same way he played — hard and to win — and although it doesn't hurt to have Stockton and Malone on your side, he certainly has been very successful. I'm sure he's as well-loved in Utah as he was in Chicago.

A client I really came to know and love, however, was John "Crash" Mengelt. John played pro ball in Cincinnati, Kansas City and Detroit before ending up with the Bulls. Jack Marin referred John to us not long after he joined the team, and our representation of him over the years has evolved into a very special and rewarding friendship.

John's wife, Linda, who was first in her class when she earned a master's in business administration from the University of Eastern Michigan, became an executive at Baxter Laboratories while John played for the Bulls. When John's career ended in 1981, he went into the executive search business with some partners, and then started his own very successful firm, which Linda ended up joining.

You won't find too many people more giving than John. On my 60th birthday, my wife and daughters had a big party for me at our tennis club. John brought a rocking chair and had everybody autograph it in black grease pencil. Then John took it and had it lacquered. It's still in my house, and one of my greatest treasures. I also have an authentic Bulls warm-up suit in my closet with my favorite number, 18, on it and my name stitched on the back. That was Bulls' guard Wilbur Hollands' jersey number when he played with John.

John's just that kind of person, very thoughtful and considerate. If he has a fault, it's that he would do anything for you and isn't always sure why everyone else isn't the same way.

When it comes to life, John and I share a similar philosophy. But our political viewpoints rarely meet. Like a lot of athletes (and other very successful people), he is a pretty staunch Republican. I think it's part of their make-up; a very strong, individualistic, I-can-do-it so why-can't-everybody-else-do-it approach.

Because we live in neighboring Chicago suburbs, John drops by the house often. Every six months or so we have this discussion on why under the Democratic administration he has to pay so much in taxes. He also wonders why I can't do something about that. I'm fond of reminding him that it's not necessarily an administration that causes high or low taxes, it's also the House Ways & Means Committee that ultimately writes these tax bills — many of the onerous taxes he's objecting to occurred under Republican administrations as well.

His wife, Linda, always looks at him and says, "John, if Harvey couldn't do anything about it the first 39 times we've discussed this, I doubt that he can do anything about it now."

Their daughter, Jennifer, it seems, might have quite a future herself. She has turned into a star volleyball player at Loyola High School. I'm still trying to push tennis on her. She'd be a natural. On a recent trip to the Mengelt's vacation home in South Carolina, she proved she too can think on her feet. She told John that someone had asked her if her father was a professional basketball player. When she told him that she had said yes, she also added a confession. She said, "Dad, I don't know how to tell you this, but I told them I was John Paxson's daughter because I wasn't sure my friends would remember you." We still have a good laugh over that one, and we've had plenty more over the years.

An April Fool's tradition somehow developed where Ellen and I would go out to dinner with John and Linda Mengelt, Tom and Linda Boerwinkle, Tate Armstrong and Tommy and Mary Lou Edwards. Tate and Tom were, of course, Bulls' players along with John, and Tommy was a Chicago disc jockey and for many years the public address voice of the Bulls. At these dinners we would raise a little bit of a ruckus, despite my efforts at being a calming influence.

With tax deadlines looming, April 1 has never been the easiest time for me, but we always managed to make time for that dinner.

I remember one year we were supposed to meet at our house and have a drink, and one-by-one they called us. I think

John called and said he couldn't make it because his garage door was broken. Then Tate called and said his car had a flat tire. Then Tommy Edwards called and said he had a flooded basement. Even before Tom Boerwinkle called and said something was wrong we had figured out the April Fool game.

Another year, the year after Tate left the Bulls, Boerwinkle and Edwards somehow borrowed a mannequin from a department store. They dressed it up in a Bulls uniform that said Tate Armstrong on the back and took it along to the restaurant with us. The mannequin got its own chair at the table, and every time the waitress came over they ordered a drink for good, old Tate. The waitress finally figured rather than argue with them, it was easier to keep bringing the mannequin drinks.

Tate was a highly regarded first pick of the Bulls who did not quite work out. He played for a couple of years and then went back out East where he's in the investment banking business. Tommy Edwards eventually moved out East as well, but now he's the program director for the CBS station in Los Angeles.

When Tom Boerwinkle finished his career with the Bulls — as probably their greatest passing center of all time — he came to my office and told me he had been released, but that former Bulls' coach Dick Motta, who had moved on to San Antonio, wanted him to come play for him down there. Tom had put on a little bit of weight from not playing, and he wanted to know what I thought of the idea.

I'm not exactly sure what I said to him, but I think I basically told him that normally he'd have nothing to lose, but he should consider whether he's in shape for the rigor at this point in his life. He did wind up giving it a shot, but soon realized his career was over. It's fitting then that his career actually ended with the Bulls because for awhile he became a great addition to their radio broadcast team, and now has a very successful career in the oil business.

Most of the athletes we've represented over the years have matured into middle and upper middle-aged successful business professionals with the same financial needs as many of our other clients. I think many agents today, despite lacking the skills of long-term financial management, insist on offering their athletes a full range of services anyway. It's a way of maintaining control over these coveted clients.

Though our practice is not built on athletes, we enjoy working with all the sports figures we represent. I hope we've served them well.

CHAPTER III
School to Work to School

The exciting and educational stimulation I've experienced on the business side of the game has been almost as gratifying as the fun I had as a sports-loving kid growing up in Chicago. As much as I craved sports, however, I quickly learned that an education was the ticket to success. By the time I was 17, I knew three things for sure: I wanted to go to college, I wanted to be a CPA and I had no money to speak of. What I needed was a plan.

A friend recommended Antioch College in Yellow Springs, Ohio. Antioch still has a reputation as one of the more progressive colleges in the country. The school also had an academic structure in which you go to school two or three semesters, and then you work one semester in a job within your career interest.

That seemed to me a pretty forward-thinking educational approach. It was also likely to be less of a financial burden than other institutions, and it would introduce me to more young people who shared my point of view. Why then did I go to the University of Wisconsin? I guess the real reason was a number of my good high school friends decided Wisconsin was the place for them. It was a great school in a great little city. So, I joined the group and headed to Madison.

They weren't readily giving out scholarships or fellowships in those days, so besides the help I got from my father I was also fortunate enough to get some help from a great aunt and two great uncles of mine. And I worked. My great aunt, Etta Nierman Schneider, was kind of the matriarch of the family, and we thought a lot alike. Because of her I am probably one of the very few men who attempted to sell hosiery on a college campus.

She carried a hosiery line in her Chicago store. She sent me some samples and I spent a semester trying to hawk them to the collegiate coeds. It didn't work very well. I don't think I was ever too enthused about the job. But I'll never forget my aunt for her kindness. These two poems, which were read at her funeral, epitomized the way she lived her life.

■ ■ ■

I shall journey through this world but once. Any good thing, therefore, that I can do, or any kindness that I can show to any human being, let me do it now; let me not neglect or defer it. For I shall not pass this way again.

N.C. Schaeffer

> At the close of life, the question will be not, how much have you got, but how much have you given; not how much have you won, but how much you have done; not how much have you saved, but how much have you sacrificed; not how much were you honored, but how much have you loved and served.
>
> N.C. Schaeffer

■ ■ ■

I liked to work, which was good, because I worked a lot through college. I worked at the *Wisconsin State Journal*, writing sports, for about a year and a half. I also waited tables and had other odd jobs at school.

The Second World War had just ended when I went up to look at the school for the first time. For those who may not remember, colleges were overflowing with applicants because all the veterans were returning to college under the G.I. Bill.

I was able to get in without any problem, but I wasn't able to get any housing — not in the dorms or anywhere else. Somehow, my friend Shelley Fink and I found a home out in Shorewood, Wisconsin — a suburb half an hour away from Madison and the campus. We rented a room in some lady's home, and I remember having to take a bus everywhere.

I don't think the lady liked us, and we didn't much care for her. She never gave us a key to the house, so we really had no freedom. We'd always have to come home at specified times so we could get in the door. After about three weeks or so, we decided this just wasn't going to work out.

We eventually found a roominghouse in the heart of campus. We each were able to get our own room. They weren't very big, but sure served our purpose.

Our friend Fred Sherman, however, was in much worse

shape. When he finally arrived at our building, the only thing left was a broom closet. Literally. They cleaned it up, stuck a cot in there, and then stuck Fred in there. I think he kept his clothes in someone else's room. I know he never changed the sheets because there wasn't enough room. He would've had to take the whole bed out just to do that, and it was a major project just getting the bed in.

Perhaps it was the close quarters that solidified our companionship, because it wasn't long after that semester that the three of us decided to join a fraternity.

Even though I've often wondered why anyone would want to join a fraternity, I did. My friends and I all joined Pi Lambda Phi, which was considered the best Jewish fraternity at the University of Wisconsin. It was just the thing to do at that time.

Our Chicago mafia group mixed mostly with people from Milwaukee and other parts of Wisconsin. I moved into the fraternity house after my first semester and stayed there for the first three years at school.

My roommates included individuals who remain my closest friends to this day: Hinks Shimberg, Shelley Fink and Barry Elman. They all became important people in my life. Hinks, whose real name is Mandell, is originally from New York but has lived for many years in Tampa, Florida. When he was living in Syracuse someone called him Hinks and it stuck. He's pretty much gone by Hinks ever since. Shelley has been the top tax lawyer at the Sonnenschein firm for many years. Barry has been my personal lawyer ever since he began practicing, and has provided me with great counsel over the years.

It was while we were roommates that Shelley met the woman who would become his wife. Now, to say he was a little carried away with Nellie would be an understatement. The rest of my friends and I quickly realized that these two were likely to get married, and that seemed to be the most popular subject in our house. We were happy for them, but we didn't need to hear about it all the time.

Shelley has always been a perfectly normal, rational and wonderful person, but the ongoing saga of his courtship got to the point that we began hiding Nellie's picture every time he mentioned her.

Nellie Weisenthal was a bit of a poster girl when she was young. At eight years of age, she left the war in Germany and traveled alone to this country to join her father, who had been here for a few years. In Germany she had lived with cousins. This courageous, blond little girl made the cover of *Newsday*. Later, when she married Shelley, I was honored to stand up in their wedding.

While Shelley found his wife early on, I never dated anyone particularly special. I spent a year or two with one young lady, but I guess I just wasn't ready to get serious. I was taken with another young lady from St. Louis, but when I visited her family down there her father made it clear to me that I didn't have enough money for her. I got the classic rebuff, but, as usual, things worked out for the best.

I certainly came to know many wonderful women at college, so my reticence toward commitment was, I'm sure, more my fault than theirs. But I was 20 years old, had no money and no definite future. I didn't know where I was going or how I was going to get there.

I didn't get married until I was 32. Hinks was also about 32 when he got married and another fraternity brother, Harold Palay, was 50 when he finally got married. So, we late bloomers formed a bit of an alliance. Hinks, especially, was always available for trips and vacations when all the married men, of course, had other commitments. Through our mutual marital delay, Hinks and I not only became very close friends, but we eventually married wonderful women. It was worth the wait.

After we graduated, Hinks went on to get his M.B.A. from Columbia University in New York. Not long after finishing at Columbia, Hinks and his brother, Jim, who is an attorney, and a third man, a builder, picked up their families lock, stock and barrel and moved from New York to Tampa, Florida.

With what turned out to be incredible insight, they partnered to become one of the most successful builders in Tampa, and one of the biggest in the state.

In 1975, I met Hinks at Chicago's O'Hare airport. He and I sat and talked for a few hours. He had just sold his business to MGIC of Milwaukee. I remember very clearly Hinks said something that I've often thought about since. He said he now had a wonderful wife, five children and enough money to pretty much do anything he wanted for the rest of his life, but he didn't know for sure what that was.

I must say, this didn't particularly shock me. I think many of us put in that position would inherit the same dilemma. We all walk around saying if I only had this and if I only had that, but if and when it comes, you are faced with the moment of truth. Okay, what do I want to do with the rest of my life both for the benefit of myself, my family and the world?

My life was consumed by family and a career as a practicing accountant when Hinks asked me to consider working with him. He was getting more involved in real estate and told me about two young Tampa businessmen who he had joined in an exciting venture. It was a project he would lead. I would manage it financially and the other two would find properties to deal — primarily apartment buildings and hotels either in Orlando or Tampa. I agreed. Our company bought the Royal Plaza Hotel in Disney World, which we sold years later. We built the Palace at Disney World, which sits just off the property and is probably the best location in Lake Buena Vista. We're still part-owners of the thousand-room hotel today.

Over the years we've done a number of things together. We've had the good fortune of investing ourselves, and having clients invest with us. All the way around, it's been a marvelous venture.

With his success, Hinks has become extremely civic-minded and is considered to be one of Tampa's most important ambassadors. He was head of the Tampa Sports Authority and led the citizens' committee to save the Buccaneers, the city's NFL football team. Hinks' wife, Elaine, is a writer of medical books. She always seems to know what's wrong with me before the doctor's do.

The Shimberg family has become a part of the Tampa landscape, and Hinks has come a long way from our days at the fraternity house. Hinks, Barry Elman, Shelley Fink and I all had a turn serving as president of the fraternity. Despite resisting what I saw as kind of a questionable goal, the members convinced me to take the helm in my junior year. Even though my daughters and my wife were all in sororities at college, and I actually became the president of a fraternity, it's still not something I spend too much time talking about.

As much as the fraternity was a part of my life at college, I had many other interests as well. In addition to covering sports for the *Wisconsin State Journal*, I spent a year as a sports writer for the university newspaper, *The Daily Cardinal*. Although writing for the papers had its advantages, an experience I had with the *Wisconsin State Journal* may have dampened my enthusiasm for pursuing that type of work in the future.

The editor sent me out one day to cover a high school baseball game. Barry Elman came along and soon wished he hadn't. I hadn't driven a car in a while and when I got to the field and realized the game was on another field, one much further down a hill, I figured I'd get there the quickest way rather than the safest.

I'm sure Barry was fearing for his life as I coasted right down the side of the hill, because a year doesn't go by without him reminding me of our four-wheel slalom.

When I wasn't studying or covering sports, you could probably find me playing sports. I played intramural football and baseball, but basketball and volleyball were the games I loved.

We had a great intramural basketball team one year, and I will go to my grave believing that a referee stole the university championship from us. We got to the semifinals of the whole university, and three of us fouled out. We lost in overtime, and I am convinced that if it wasn't a religious vendetta on the part of the referee, then he just didn't know what he was doing.

Volleyball was probably my best sport, though, and I think we lost in the finals there too. Shelley played on the team with me. He was a great athlete on Wisconsin's basketball team and a star on their baseball team, setting a Big 10 record at third base with no errors in 95 chances througout an entire season. He turned down a minor league offer from the Philadelphia Phillies — at the time the money wasn't that great, and he had a mind for law.

In any case, he was a great volleyball set-up man all season, but he had a final exam the day after our championship game.

He needed to study, and we sure missed him that day. That's the only time in my life I've ever really been angry at him.

I got involved in playing bridge at college. To this day I play a monthly game with my business partner Steve, Marty Salzman and Dr. Paul Willis. (He took our good friend Erv Imrem's place when he passed away a few years ago. Erv was one of Steve's special friends and his death was tough on all of us in every way.) Because I had early morning classes and late afternoon classes, I'd often spend the middle of the day playing at the house bridge table. A friend named Jack Oppenheim became my playing partner. In my last semester, we actually won the University of Wisconsin bridge championship — it was the same week when the city championship was going on and a number of players were across town playing in that, but we still basked in our victory.

If you were to ask me what the greatest "fun" high was in my four years at Madison . . . well, I'd probably say playing basketball, but a close second would be an experience I had in a psychology class at the school's Bascom Hall. Bascom Hall sits at the top of a famous hill in the city. Walking up that hill in the cold of winter on my way to a lecture in psychology was a brutal experience, but one day it was well worth it.

The professor decided to conduct what he considered a "psychological experiment." He had the whole class stand up, a few hundred students at least, and then he would randomly read off a list of numbers starting, I believe, with seven. From there you would have to repeat the numbers back. If you didn't get it right, you had to sit down.

Well, after seven, eight, nine numbers there were still plenty of us standing. But by ten most of the class was seated. At twelve there were three of us left, and at thirteen there were two. I got thirteen, and the other person dropped out. I was all alone up there, and I missed on fourteen numbers. I reversed two numbers, but it was a proud moment.

I've always had somewhat of a photographic memory with numbers, and a natural capacity to figure out where numbers belong. That classroom experience, along with a few other reasons, helped confirm my desire to be a CPA.

The very first time I went into my Accounting 101 class, the professor looked at all of us — it was a very large class — and said, "I'm not sure what any of you are ever going to get out of this class, but if you don't remember another thing I tell you, then just remember this. As an accountant or as a businessman, never anticipate a profit."

I've tried to remember that, and I think it's served me well. I don't know what happened to that fine gentleman, but I appreciate the wisdom.

My summer breaks from college were spent working with a man I had already learned to appreciate. Herb Greenwald needed a summer-time accountant for his business, and I needed accounting experience. Herb had started a construction and development company in Chicago named Herbert Realty, which became Metropolitan Structures. But I had met him long before all of this, when he was the principal of Ner Tamid Congregation Hebrew Elementary and High School.

It was really my mother who thought I ought to attend Hebrew High School. I wasn't too crazy about the idea. But Herb made the adjustment easier, and became an instrumental person in my life.

Herb was in his late 30s at the time. He was smart, handsome and spoke seven or eight different languages. A man of his intellect must have gotten bored from time to time because I remember him having contests determining the fastest reader. I always won and I don't think he ever asked if

I knew what I was reading, that wasn't part of the game. He seemed to become somewhat of a fan of mine, and I was certainly a fan of his.

My mother bumped into Herb while I was away at college my first year. She discovered his new venture and then he asked what I was doing in the summer. From then on, I was fortunate to have a summer job that taught me the ropes.

In fact, when I graduated from college, I spent a whole year working for Herb. This was just before I joined the Navy, and wound up being stationed in Washington, D.C. Herb used to come into town and we'd go out to dinner together. Not long after that, he was killed at a tragically young age. He died in the East River in New York when the altimeter failed on an American Airlines' plane.

I've never forgotten Herb and all the adventures that came with working for him. Starting from virtually nothing, he became one of the premier builders and developers in Chicago. He became associated with Mies Van Der Rohe, the world-famous architect, and together they built modern glass and steel buildings. They built Sherman Gardens Apartments in Evanston, the buildings at 860 and 880 Lake Shore Drive downtown, the Twin Tower Apartments in Hyde Park and many more.

He was, for many reasons, the most unforgettable person I've ever met. For a man of such immense brilliance, he sure had some peculiar idiosyncrasies. I remember he would always race out to the airport with no time to spare. Before one particular trip, he quickly said to me, "I need some money for cabs." I handed him $20. When he came back from New York he said to me, "Don't you ever do that again." What? He said, "You gave me money, and you never got a receipt for it." I said, I know, but you didn't have time. He tells me that doesn't matter, that there is no excuse.

About two-three weeks later, he again asks me for some money. I say, here, sign this. He says I don't have time to sign and I tell him you don't get any money until you sign it. He gets really angry, and says, "Look, I know what I said, but give me the money. I've got to go." I wouldn't give it to him, and he finally signed the receipt.

I could get away with those kind of things because he really liked me, and because I knew deep down that my work for him was only temporary, that I'd move on before long.

The full year after college during which I worked for Herb came about because, although I was accepted into the Navy, they had found a minor cyst that had to be removed before I could get into the service. That gave me more time with Herb, which was okay be me because the Korean War was just heating up.

During that time, a young lawyer named Ira Kipnis began working for us and I remember one day Herb just laying him out over God knows what. You could hear his voice booming through the whole office.

I know Ira well and he's a very bright, independent and successful man. To his credit, I think that was the last day he worked for Herb. But Herb was that way. He was tough, and the man just never slept. The chances of him being in the office at three o'clock every morning were as good as him not being there. He used to change secretaries on a whim and then hire them back because he knew he needed them. If they didn't have a flower waiting for his lapel every day, that would probably be enough reason to be fired, but he was a spectacular, brilliant person, charming as can be.

His early death was just a tragedy. His whole family was wonderful, it was a great pleasure to know them. The years I worked for Herb I wouldn't trade for anything.

With the Korean War going on, those of us who graduated college, were healthy and didn't have any visible means of deferment were faced with some, in my opinion, Hobson's choices.

I could have gotten drafted, of course, or could have tried to apply for a commission somewhere. I couldn't have been a pilot, and I didn't like the army. I also could have tried for the marines, like Hinks Shimberg.

Hinks joining the marines really blew my mind at the time, and also gave me a whole new level of respect for him — even though he may have set the corps back a couple of years. I remember watching him in Washington on Fridays when they did their famous close-order drills.

My option turned out to be the Navy. I applied for officer candidate school, was accepted pending that minor surgery and after finishing up with Herb — at the ripe, old age of 22 — I found myself ready to join the United States Navy.

I had a few hundred dollars to my name, bought a used red Dodge and one day just said good-bye to my family and drove that Dodge to Newport, Rhode Island, for what was nine weeks of officer candidate training school.

I'll never forget that trip, partly because the car leaked. Rain water was coming through the hood and soaking my feet. I remember grabbing a hat I had with me and — out there on the Pennsylvania/New Jersey Turnpikes on the way to Newport — driving with the hat on top of my foot in order to keep the top of the gas pedal dry. This was the routine for most of the trip.

I arrived in Newport and got ready for what turned out to be a most unpleasant nine weeks. I never really adjusted well to new situations like this, and I wasn't very fired up about being part of the military in any form. I've always felt that had my time come later when the Vietnam War was on, I would have had a real struggle with myself as to whether or not to become a conscientious objector or go to Canada. I never had to answer that question so I don't know what I would have done.

If the military and I were incompatible, it didn't help that about 95% of the other candidates for officership were from the fleet, and very few of us were from civilian life. So, it wasn't only that it was something new, but that it was something newer to me than almost everybody else.

I remember clearly I had a lot of trouble sleeping those weeks, and sometimes I just walked the barracks. There was another fellow, Justin Bereny, who not only had trouble sleeping then, but still does. He's out in California now, and we've stayed close friends over all these years. I didn't sleep because I didn't like the adjustment. He didn't sleep because that's how he lived his life. We became very close friends and ended up in Washington together for most of the time. I proceeded to try and make the best that I could out of the Navy.

One of the requirements at OCS was that you took exams all the time. There were eight courses. There were two exams for each course each week, and you had to get 125 total in each of the courses, which means you had to average a 62.5. That sounds reasonable for an intelligent person, but if you're new to something, and you're trying to learn eight courses in one week, it's not quite so easy.

I remember the first time I took the exam on insignias and emblems. I just didn't have time to study. I guess I didn't realize that was going to be that much of the test. I got a 25. That meant I had to get a hundred on the next test that week in that course. Well, you might say, what's the big deal? They're not going to flunk you out, which may or may not have been true, but the reward for passing all your courses in a week was that you got off on Sunday and went to Providence, Rhode Island, which was about an hour's ride from Newport.

Sure enough, I stopped studying everything else that week and actually got a 100 on the second part of that course's exams, and was able to get to Providence over the weekend. I got a hotel room and tried to get some sleep so I could get through the next week.

If my memory is correct, out of the whole class I was the only one who managed to get at least 125 in every course every week. I didn't finish at the top, but I was able to balance things out enough so that I at least got my Sundays off for nine weeks. When I got there they gave us a bunch of aptitude tests with numbers and letters and things like that, and except for the spatial exams I would be done in half the time of everybody else — which did me no good at all, of course. I just had to sit around and wait for everybody else to finish. So certain things came easy to me, but it took me two weeks to learn how to make the bunks right so I didn't get points off on inspection.

One of my least favorite memories is that everyone had to jump into a pool off of a high diving tower, and this was in the middle of winter. It had to be below zero and we weren't allowed to put on jackets. We walked two or three blocks from our barracks to the pool. I don't love heights in general, and I didn't love jumping into pools from such a height. Somehow I managed to convince them that I had a bad cold, which I probably did along with everybody else, and I remember getting out of that jump. Everybody got out of the pool, got back into their clothes and walked back in the middle of the winter. Half of the barracks was sick for the next two to three weeks.

I suppose that's part of the training, but it never made much sense to me. I did, however, finish the nine weeks and graduate.

I was 22 when I completed the course at Newport. At that time officer ensigns, such as myself, all went to the next stop, which was five months in Bayonne, New Jersey, to learn how to be a supply officer. Today I believe the training is held in Augusta, Georgia. I think we were the last or the next-to-last class that went to Bayonne, which was fine. It was a great five months. Bayonne is half an hour from New York. We had a lot of free time, and learning to be a supply officer was nothing like the boot camp of Newport.

Justin Bereny and I were close friends by that point. We took an apartment together in Bayonne, and I remember I played a lot of softball. I was the starting pitcher on the officers' team, 12-inch fast-ball pitching. We won often, a lot more than we lost. We had a fellow officer on the team named Frank Brower, who I will never forget. He was smart, good-looking and women loved him. We used to go into New York City, and I don't know about the rest of us but he had all the women following him.

At the end of our stay in Bayonne, we had to decide and apply for where we wanted to spend the next two-and-a-half years of our three-year enlistment. The war was pretty close to ending, but there was still a certain amount of significant danger out there if you were in the fleet. I had done very well at supply school, and I decided to apply for a post in Washington, D.C., never dreaming I would get it because most of us got scattered all over the face of the earth.

That reminds me of comedian Steven Wright's story. He said he had the greatest collection of seashells. He had so many of them he had to keep them strewn over all the beaches of the world. Well, that's what happened to our class. We got strewn over all the beaches of the world. But Justin and I both applied for assignment in Washington, D.C., and amazingly enough were both assigned there. We were, I think, the only two that got sent to Washington. I became a commissary officer for three naval bases in D.C., and Justin became an officer at one of the civilian type facilities.

Comparatively, I had a lot to do and he had nothing to do. He literally spent two-and-a-half years just signing his name when he was told to. He did a lot of reading. I always thought that was a clear example of the waste that goes on in both the government and the military. I mean there was a perfectly bright, energetic, ambitious, willing-to-work type person who couldn't find anything to do. It would have driven me crazy, but he managed to put up with it.

I don't know a lot about food. Fortunately my wife does so our family eats very well, but I didn't need to cook for my detail. I did, however, need to be sure our galleys were properly run since we were responsible for feeding all the Navy facilities in Washington — that included our base, a gun factory base and a third base, Anacostia. We were also responsible for providing all the food to the White House. President Eisenhower was in office then, and I remember every day we would send food over to the White House. His chefs, of course, would do the cooking.

One of the bonuses in my job was that I was one of about three or four male officers who had unlimited access to the Anacostia base since I had to be there to check on the galleys and on the food service. That's where all the Waves were, and there were a few of them that I spent more time with than just making sure they were fed properly. But again nothing significant or noteworthy happened. I got out of there sane and single with no problems.

I lived at 532 20th Street, NW, which was right next to the Red Cross building in northwest Washington. Washington, of course, is one of the great cities of the world. I just loved all two and a half years there, although I was getting kind of restless and really had had enough of the Navy long before I was through. But it was a very exciting city in a very exciting time. There were always things to do and we took advantage of that. I remember 50 of us were picked out of the area to serve as escorts for the famous Cherry Blossom Festival that they have every spring. We escorted the 50 women, one from each state, who were going to be the cherry blossom queens.

Despite what you might guess, that was not one of the great experiences of my life. We were lined up by height, all 50 of us, and then the women we were matched with stood opposite us. I ended up with some young lady who was a daughter of a congressman from Maryland who I believe went to Barnard. It's not quite fair to say that there were 49 good-looking women and the congressman's daughter, but that was close, and that would have been all right if we got along, but for some reason she didn't seem to like me, and I didn't like her any better. Whether I wasn't a likely candidate for her future or she just didn't like people in general, or me in particular, I don't know, but what should have been a great experience was not. I spent a whole weekend escorting her around, and she said three civil words.

My more natural routine was to come home, eat dinner out most likely and then not eat again until the next morning. For a year and a half straight I went into the base first thing in the morning and had a cup or two, at least, of black Navy coffee out of a huge cauldron that was making coffee for the whole base, and a French-fried donut right out of the greasy grills. I finally noticed that I was having a problem with my stomach. I went for some tests at Bethesda Naval Hospital in Maryland. They found I had a small duodenal ulcer, so they put me in the hospital for about three or four days and then released me. About a month later I took some more tests and found out I was fine and haven't had any trouble since then. To this day, the only thing I can't drink or eat is a cup of black coffee or a French-fried donut, which is probably more psychosomatic than physical. I remember calling home and telling my folks that I was going to be in the hospital for a few days. My father flew out just to make sure I was all right. It's amazing, the things we remember and the significant incidents in our lives.

I know things weren't financially much better than they ever had been for my father at that time. He had to be in his 40s and had run through a few publishing-type jobs, none of which seemed to work out very well.

Somewhere in that time I remember him telling me he took a handful of dimes, went to a pay phone one Sunday morning (why not at home I don't know) — he must have had 50 dimes — and took out the industrial "want ads" or "for sale" sections for machinery, equipment and property that the *Chicago Tribune* ran. He sat there and called all the people who had advertised, or at least as many as he could afford to call. He told them he had this newspaper that specialized in the sale of industrial equipment, machinery and property, and he literally, with no more than a handful of dimes and nowhere to work, built a business called Industrial Market Place.

Since then, a couple of other publications have been added, but that's how it all started. I guess if necessity is the mother of invention, he was just on his last ropes, and yet somehow his determination and his drive enabled him to convince people to go with him.

I'm sure he didn't get very good results at first. All he probably did was send it out to a few hundred plants somewhere, but it grew and grew, and now it's a very important part of that game. It is now the leading publication on industrial auctions and many other things, with 140 to 150 pages per issue. It is published every other week. It's been a business that's taken good care of my folks and my brother and his family for years.

But at the time he came out to visit me in the hospital, I said to myself I know he can't afford to do this. That's why it meant so much more to me.

But that was the climate of the times. So for the first year and a half I was the commissary officer, and then with a year to go they made me fiscal officer, which got me into something that I was not only familiar with but that I could also do well. For the last year of my service in Washington I was the fiscal officer for the whole Naval base, which meant budgeting and reporting and accounting and things like that.

Finally, at the ripe, old age of 25, my three years in the service were up. I was honorably discharged as a Lieutenant, J.G. I got in the same old car that got me there, it had stopped leaking by then, and drove back to Chicago ready to start what was going to be the rest of my life — whatever that was.

This is me at a very young age with my grandmother, great-grandfather and father. A nice four-generation picture.

Mom and Dad

The whole family in our backyard.

I couldn't ask for better sons-in-law.

My brother Joel and I have always been close.

That's my oldest friend, Burt Joseph, and me when we were somewhat younger. Burt is now a renowned first amendment lawyer.

Allan Muchin and me in one of my favorite pictures.

(Top left) Hinks Shimberg, of Tampa, Florida, and I have had a long and successful run together. (Top right) World famous neurosurgeon Dr. Leonard Cerullo and I have been working together for more than 25 years. (Top center) Shelley Fink and I have played plenty of games since this picture.

The Minors (left), Ellen and me and the Muchins.

Three of Bobby Hull's sons joined him and me at the press conference announcing his unprecedented contract with the Winnipeg Jets. That was a big day for all of us. At the far right is Gary Davidson, the WHA chairman.

CHICAGO DAILY NEWS, Wednesday, July 5, 1972

Insight

Accountant Wineberg helped the Golden Jet to work out world's biggest sports contract

How Bobby Hull iced a fortune

By Bill Christine

Harvey S. Wineberg, certified public accountant, sports devotee, sometime tennis player and a man who hangs out professionally on the 15th floor of the Sherman building, occupies a warm, comfortable office that brings up the rear of a maze of business suites.

"I'll be your guide to Mr. Wineberg," says a girl at the front door.

Late last February, Ben Hatskin, a middle-aged man whose manifold interests leapfrog from football to juke boxes to high-priced hockey players, found his way back to Wineberg's desk.

Whether Hatskin's mission was suicidal or not will be determined by the hourglass. The moment he slipped into a chair across from Wineberg, however, the biggest sports deal in the history of money was under way.

TECHNICALLY, BOBBY HULL'S fortune hunt began the previous November, when the Black Hawks were in Vancouver at the same time as Hatskin, who was there for Canada's Grey Cup championship football game.

Hatskin spoke briefly with Hull, mentioning a new hockey league, a franchise in Winnipeg and a million dollars.

The last two items contained responsive rings for Hull, who contacted Wineberg, his financial adviser of the past year, once the Hawks returned to Chicago.

"Let's not do anything yet," Wineberg told Hull. "They'll get to us if they're serious."

SO NOW IT WAS FEBRUARY and Hatskin, after a preliminary phone call, was the mountain come to Mohammed, sitting vis-a-vis with Wineberg.

"We'd like a million dollars," Wineberg said, and for Hatskin it must have sounded like an echo.

"Where will I get a million dollars?" the Winnipeg man asked.

Thinking a moment, Hatskin finally said: "Maybe I could get it from the league."

"Maybe you could," Wineberg said.

Harvey Wineberg

"We'd like a million dollars."

HULL AND WINEBERG and the world discovered that Hatskin's words were deeds, that the Winnipeg owner wasn't talking in mirages. It St. Paul, cidadel of the embroyonic World Hockey Assn., Hull was presented a cashier's check from the United California Bank, Santa Ana branch, for $1 million, and hours later, in Winnipeg, the Golden Jet signed a 10-year contract which means an additional, guaranteed $1.75 million. Tallying up the $2.75 million lode can't be done with an abacus.

It was a deal that wasn't hammered out until Hull, Wineberg, Hatskin, lawyers for all parties and Gary Davidson, president of the WHA, agreed on a compendium of legalese. The result of their labors is a 13-page contract with World Hockey Assn. Properties Inc. (for $1 million) and a 26-page contract with the Winnipeg Jets (for the rest).

The first cool million already is Hull's. "I went to have a copy of the check made, and the girl almost had a heart attack," Wineberg said. The balance, at the rate of $250,000 for the next five years, then at $100,000 for the final five years, won't start coming Hull's way until Oct. 1, the day after a four-year contract with the Black Hawks expires.

Surprisingly, Hull's ultimate deal is, amost to the penny, the same as it was spelled out when Davidson and Wineberg met here in late March.

Along the way, though, there were loopholes to be sewn up, and sometimes the loopholes had loopholes. The complexities of the legal documents, secured in a gray filing case in Wineberg office, would stagger the neophyte.

In writing, for instance, it gives Hull the right to coach the Winnipeg team, or quit coaching any time he wishes. Regarding the arrangement with World Hockey Assn. Properties Inc. (WHAP), a California entity, the moneys are to be split between the corporation and Hull, with a larger amount going to the side that initiates the particular endorsement opportunity.

THE ENDORSEMENT ARRANGEMENT covers a wide range of commercial products, athletic equipment as well as personal appearances by Hull.

"From the start," Wineberg said, "we questioned Hatskin regarding the assurance that if Bobby signed he would be playing for Winnipeg and not another team in the league. I don't believe the man ever thought of drafting Bobby, signing him and then perhaps having him play somewhere else. And in all our dealings with him, he hasn't lied to us yet."

The particulars of the contract would make it difficult for

Turn to Page 6, Column 1

A 1972 article in the *Chicago Daily News* featured details of the above signing.

Jack Marin was one of the first Chicago Bulls to become a client. He sent me this photo and signed it, "To Harvey; Largely because of your efforts, I can now turn my back on the NBA. Many, many thanks. Jack."

John Paxson (left) and John Mengelt (right) are two former Bulls who became both clients and close friends.

Beltin' Bill Melton was the 1971 American League home run champ. He's also been and still is a great client.

Leo (left) and his assistant coach Joe Amalfitano (right) were nice enough to let me wear a Cubs' uniform at spring training one year. Leo gave me this photo and wrote, "If you could only hit. Thanks for being a real friend."

The young man on the left, Leo Durocher, went on to become a great client and better friend. The guy on the right, of course, is the one and only Babe Ruth.

This is me in Buenos Aires, in 1995, where I represented the U.S. in the Maccabi Games.

That's Tim Gullikson at Wimbledon. He sent this photo to me and wrote, "To Harvey, the guy with the huge forehand!"

Working on U.S. Sen. Paul Simon's campaign was a rich and rewarding experience.

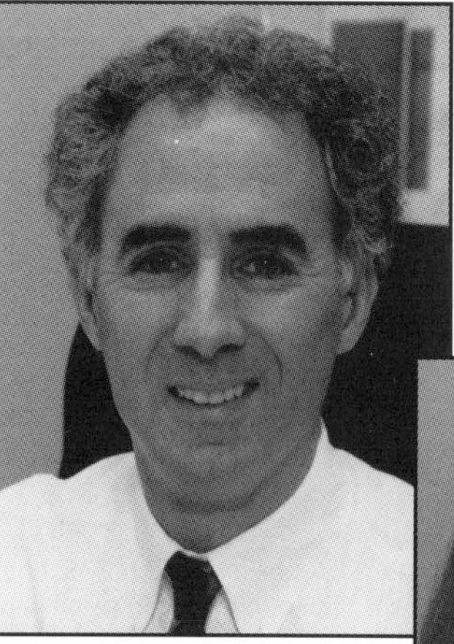

When I met Steve Lewis at Camp Ojibwa in Eagle River, Wisconsin, I had little idea we'd become long-time partners.

Ellen (center) with Gail and Arnie Heltzer.

At a fundraiser for Illinois Senator Dick Durbin, Ellen and I were able to meet President Clinton. But we couldn't stay long, our daughter was giving birth at the same time.

The early days with Triangle Productions meant working closely with the popular singing group, The Chad Mitchell Trio.

Another music man, jazz legend Ramsey Lewis, became a client later and is still a close friend and wonderful talent.

Through Leo, Ellen and I were invited to a birthday party for Frank Sinatra. Right before this picture was taken, Frank said, "Nobody smile." So we didn't.

CHAPTER IV
Father and Son

As you can tell, I had a tremendous amount of respect and admiration for my father, Henry Wineberg. He was one of the truly caring people in the world, and rather than just talk about it, he did things for people. Whether it was the family or politics or social organizations, he was instrumental in making things happen.

Not everyone agreed with my father all of the time, but they saw him as a man of strong character and principle. So, when it came time for me to decide what I was going to embark upon, I had a certain amount of guilt relating to him, and to the struggles and triumphs he experienced in his long business career.

When I was born in 1930, my father worked for the old *Chicago Herald Examiner*, a Hearst owned newspaper that later became the *Chicago Daily News* before eventually going out of business. He graduated from Northwestern University's School of Journalism, and worked on the financial pages in some capacity. He was an active member of the union that went on strike against the Hearst empire.

They were on strike for, I think, close to two years, one of the longest newspaper strikes in the history of the country. It was not an easy time.

Between the Depression, a newborn baby and the amount of time my dad was out there fighting the Hearsts, my mother certainly had her hands full.

My mother wasn't much for politics. She operated on her instincts, and perhaps these differences kept my parents from true compatibility. But that's just the way their life turned out.

The strike was eventually settled, but there were no winners. My father turned to the publishing business not long after that. He spent some time with *Advertising Age*, and then he and a partner, Herb Simon, bought *Baseball Digest*.

While the publication still exists, the partnership didn't last long. My father and Herb had a falling out and, after my father was bought out, he held various positions at different publishing companies in the city. These jobs didn't always amount to too much, and that put some strain on our family.

Despite many years of struggle, my father never surrendered his principles, and never gave up on his own business aspirations. Those aspirations eventually led him to run Industrial Market Place, the publishing company which still thrives today under the leadership of my younger brother, Joel.

We had some wealthy relatives, and that probably made things even tougher for my mother to accept. We didn't have a car or television until I was 19. That seems hard to believe today, that a "middle class" family would be without a television.

When we finally did get a car, I managed to bang it into the garage door the very first day we got it. The garage was small and the area behind it narrow, so it could be difficult to maneuver if you didn't know what you were doing.

I do remember a rare occasion when my father showed up at one of my baseball games. I saw him standing behind a tree, watching. He never told me he was there, but I saw him. One of his proudest moments, I remember, was taking me to Soldier Field at a very young age to hear President Franklin Roosevelt speak. Roosevelt was always one of my dad's heroes.

I was born on what people call the "great" West Side of Chicago. In those days it was more of a Jewish neighborhood, while today the great majority of its residents are black. Though it's not far from the western suburb of Oak Park, which has become a model for interracial living — much like Evanston on the North Side — it's a low-income neighborhood that's struggled from the social tragedy of poverty and segregation. I still drive by my old neighborhood on occasion, but it's very sad to see the struggle that remains.

When I was nine, our family moved to the West Rogers Park neighborhood on the North Side. One of my earliest and oldest friends from the Austin neighborhood is Burt Joseph, who is now a topflight lawyer, an expert in obscenity law and counsel to *Playboy* magazine. Later in life he and his wife, Babs, introduced me to the American Civil Liberties Union, which I've been involved with for more than 25 years.

I'm not sure if Burt remembers this or not, but I was at his family's house one day when some kind of an argument started. I threw a yo-yo across the room and hit Burt's brother, Jack, splitting open his forehead. Who knows why I did something like that, but I happened to talk to Jack on the phone recently and I'm glad to report the yo-yo incident caused him no long-term damage.

I'm sure that's as violent as I've ever gotten. Most of my time as a kid was spent with a ball in my hand. Everybody would comment that the only thing I wanted to do was play ball. I did turn into a fairly good athlete, nothing great, but there are a lot of athletic genes on both my mother's and my father's sides of the family.

My mother's oldest brother, Harry Steinberg, was a great basketball player at Lane Tech High School back in the 1930s. I once saw an old newspaper article on the city championship game he played in. Harry scored two points, but it was the only basket of the game. It's hard to believe that's possible with the game we know today, but the city championship game was won two to nothing.

My brother, Joel, was born when I was seven. He's my only sibling, and at the time I remember being relieved that my mother didn't have a girl. A little girl is certainly not anything a little boy wants at that point in his life. I'd walk around our apartment building telling everyone it was going to be a boy, and that if it was a girl I was just going to throw her out. There's no way I would have a little sister.

I ended up not only with a brother who was a great friend as a kid, but a brother who, once we both got through school and military service, has been a great friend and integral part of my adult life.

The West Rogers Park neighborhood of today is also far different than it was when I grew up there. At that time it was literally a wilderness. Two blocks from our house was farmland and prairie, and I remember it being kind of a traumatic move.

Somewhere along the way my mother and her family had inherited enough money to buy a nice six-flat apartment building in Rogers Park. We lived on the second floor, and just a couple of blocks away was Clinton Grammar School.

I went to Clinton for three years and met Sy Levin, my best friend for a long, long time. We became inseparable. Besides being a terrific person, Sy was probably one of the best athletes in the city. He lived just two blocks west of me, and playing ball was what we did.

Ironically, in eighth grade we were the two final candidates for mayor of the school, and I honestly never thought I had a chance to beat him. He was one of those all-around, special people. I must have done something right because about an hour before they were supposed to announce the winner someone stuck their head into my gym class and whispered to me that I had won. It was one of the nicest moments in my life because Sy had won everything else up until then. I guess I had one coming.

I also apparently had one coming when Mrs. Beers, my sixth grade teacher, threw an eraser at me that hit me in the head. I was okay, but I didn't know what provoked her. I was a good student and a good person in school, but I must have done something she didn't like.

I remember going home that night and mentioning it to my folks — it was one of the few nights my father was home for dinner — and sure enough he was there the next day. I don't think he tore up the school, but I'm sure he got some kind of satisfaction.

After school, of course, there were games to be played. I played third base on the baseball team and was a guard on our basketball team. I wasn't a bad tennis player either, but most kids in those days just played team sports, so I never took up tennis seriously. I have played a lot of tennis in the last half of my life though, and sometimes I regret not really learning it when I was young.

On the streets —Francisco Avenue to be exact — we played line ball. It's hard to believe we got away with this game, but line ball is like stick ball. If you hit the ball past one car, you had a single, past the next car, you had a double and so on.

Of course, we also played 16-inch softball, Windy City Ball, in the city that invented the game. We'd mix the two games, go out into the street and hit softballs. If you hit a car, that was all right. It was legal. Breaking the window was not, but we didn't seem to do much of that. I can't believe that somebody didn't stop us from playing in the street and causing dents in cars all over the place, but that's what life was like.

I remember I would eat dinner with my feet out from under the table, and within minutes I'd be out of the house and have some kind of game going. Sometimes we'd go over to the school yard and play pinners. If we couldn't get a baseball game going, we'd stick a net up in the middle of the street and play soccer or street hockey. We were always doing something, and that's missing from what kids do today.

Now, that's not to say I never got into any trouble. I sneaked out of the house one night. I was supposed to stay in, but I went over to meet my friend, Jordie Krugel, and for some reason he was picking up a floor lamp in his apartment and trying to move it from one end of the room to the other. He hit me in the mouth and chipped my front tooth, which has since been bonded. I went home and my mother, of course, wasn't extremely happy about that. I told her I had fallen down and chipped it. I don't lie very well, but that just seemed to me a little white lie that was easy to live with. I'm not sure if she ever learned the truth.

If lying didn't come easy for me, school did. If I didn't win every spelling bee, I won practically every spelling bee. And math contests, even better. I know I won all of those. I ended up graduating Hebrew school at the same time I graduated grammar school. I eventually graduated from Hebrew High School as well. On the High Holidays I can still sit in the temple and read everything, but I don't know what I'm reading anymore than I did then.

While grammar school was in the neighborhood, a long bus ride took me to Nicholas Senn High School. In 1943, Senn was the only main high school on the North Side of Chicago, taking freshmen from West Rogers Park all the way over to the lake and down into the Lakeview neighborhood. The only other high school nearby was Sullivan, which was somewhat further north along the lake, coincidentally where my wife Ellen went to school.

I would say that my four years at Senn High School were semi-distinguished in an undistinguished way, or maybe distinguished in a semi-distinguished way. I did well in all respects, but I don't think I'm written up in any of the annals of the famous people who graduated from Senn.

Among the high points was finishing 18th in a class of 243. I also managed to get the only F that I've ever gotten in a course anywhere, in art. I never quite understood why if you went to the classes and did the work, just because you had no artistic talent, a teacher should give you an F.

I became sports editor of the Senn Bulldog newspaper in my senior year and covered a lot of games. One of the sad parts of the experience was that I was never on the basketball team. I always thought I should have been.

The summer before tryouts I would go over to Sy Levin's house on the edge of the wilderness and practice. We had a basket nailed up to a tree. There was no court, just trampled down dirt that wasn't just uneven, but very bumpy. I always felt I had to look at the ground while I was practicing, and during the tryouts that stayed with me. I got on the floor and watched the ground instead of where I was going. I stopped, hit a shot from somewhere and the coach, Cap Leighton, a legend at Senn for tennis and basketball, called me over and said you can't play that way. You're not on the team. That was kind of a sad moment for me, and I believe my last year there we were city champs, led by Whitey Pearson, an all-city basketball player.

In those days there were some racial problems at the school. There were a lot of incidents between Italians and Jews and some involving Blacks. The school decided to start a club called the Green & White Club — the school colors. The club was supposed to try to exert some leadership by representing all the various ethnic factions.

I was honored when I was asked to join in my senior year. I was also a member of a fraternity called the Iaeta's. Again, God knows why anybody in high school — or anywhere else for that matter — would want to join a fraternity. But there I was, and I became its president. I don't know if we ever did anything good, but we had some fun. I spent three or four years of my life with that group.

I will never forget the initiation. The paddling was really brutal, and I came home one night and thought my mother was going to go right to the hospital after taking a look at the various colors that I exhibited. There was a fellow named Frank Epstein, who ended up playing starting guard for Notre Dame's football team and was as tough as they come, and even he found it to be almost more than he could bear. If I remember correctly, either we stopped the tradition or the school stopped it.

While there were plenty of sports, studies and social

groups in my high school life, I can't say that there were any special young women to speak of. By then I had grown to about six feet, and I guess there are no reasons why I shouldn't have had a number of girlfriends, but either I wasn't ready for them or I lacked the confidence. I went out a number of times, but that wasn't a big part of my life.

At about this age, most of my friends went to summer camp. Many of them went to a camp up in Eagle River, Wisconsin, called Camp Ojibwa. It is not only the best known camp, but the best camp in the Midwest.

My parents could never afford to send me to camp. Although I heard a lot of great things about it, I can't say I was jealous because I didn't know what I was missing. As life would have it, I ended up marrying the daughter of the man who started the camp, Al Schwartz. He owned it for 58 years, but then, with my help, he ended up selling it.

One summer I did go up to Wisconsin. I went as a junior counselor to a camp called Camp Flambeau, which wasn't quite as good as Ojibwa athletically, but was a fine camp. And I didn't have to pay for anything. I didn't get paid anything, either, but I had a great summer. I remember with perfect clarity being the best basketball player at camp. It gave me a chance to play every day. I'd be out there four or five hours a day and just get into one of those mini-zones, but when I left there somehow it never developed beyond that.

My experience at Camp Flambeau was enlightening, and one event stands out in my mind. The senior counselor in my cabin was a man named Hermie Goodman. I remember being kind of a leader in the junior counselor group, and everything seemed to be going my way. Toward the end of the summer Hermie called me over and said, I want to tell you something, and I don't want you to ever forget it. He said you are one of the most outstanding young men I've ever known, but you are not taking full advantage of your capacities and your capabilities. He also said you should somehow find a way to concentrate and be even better than you are. Not everyone has the chance to take advantage of their abilities like you do, and I don't think you're putting out the way you really ought to.

I don't know if that ever affected my life or not. I would guess somewhere it must have or I still wouldn't remember it. I don't know what happened to Hermie, but I'll never forget him giving me advice that was as helpful and constructive as any advice I've ever received.

For the most part, I kind of hung around in the summers. If you were a ball player in the city of Chicago in those days, you could stay busy every day and night playing something, and that's what I did.

I also kept up with family events. As a kid I most vividly remember the family trips we used to make to the South Side of Chicago. We'd take a bus to the El and then another bus from there to my Great-Aunt Etta's house. She lived with my great grandfather, Moses Nierman, on Hyde Park Boulevard. Every year the whole family would go there for seders — that's the Passover seder that celebrates the Jews exodus from Egypt — and all of my cousins and uncles and aunts and great-uncles and great-aunts would be there. I'm sure there were 35 to 40 people at these events, and they were kind of fun. It didn't ever seem to bother me that we didn't have a car because if you're not used to something, you just don't miss it that much. Of course, it was a long ride back after all that food, but certainly worth it for all the time shared with family.

When I got out of the service my dad needed some help with his business. With all the sacrifices he made to help get me through college, I felt I at least owed him that. I also owed it to myself to see if this business might be something that made sense for me.

The business was run out of a storefront about half-a-mile from our house. I lived at home while working there, and the most exciting thing that happened while I was there was probably also the scariest.

We discovered some sort of acrid gas in the air. We couldn't figure out where it was coming from so we brought in some specialists to check it out. Someone eventually concluded that we used a printing ink in the office that apparently would seep into wooden partitions in the wall. In the winter, the wood sucked the gas in. In the summer, the wood would expand and push the gas into the air. No one got really sick, but it was not a healthy environment to work in until we fixed it.

Working together every day brought us closer. I was at an age where I spent a lot of time thinking about the world and my place in it. I remember taking some walks with my father after dinner. We'd discuss the big issues that were on my mind, but it always came back to the same question: we'd wonder whether or not people were basically good. It's obviously a crucial question, one which determines what kind of world we live in and what our future holds.

I have no doubt that people are born good, but can then be negatively affected by society. I'm sure there are genetic exceptions, but life's obstacles can certainly exert extreme pressure on those of us who lack a solid support system.

Between working with my father and tackling these big questions, I also rekindled my friendship with Sy Levin. We were both finished with college and out of the service. I remember going to his brother's house one night. Sy's brother Mort was an executive at Krochs & Company, a large book store chain, and the most well-read person I'd ever known. We were talking to Mort about life and careers and I remember him saying there is really no substitute for the feeling that you've done something on your own. This is not to say that people who go into a business or into a profession that's established shouldn't have a feeling of accomplishment or of making something bigger or better or more meaningful, but to this day I take great pride in the fact that I literally started with nothing and built something that has been fulfilling for me and, hopefully, important to others.

I kept Mort's comments in the back of my mind for a while. After about two years with my father's business I realized that although I had a bit of it in my blood, publishing wasn't what I wanted to do with the rest of my life.

In fact, I had never given up on the idea that I was really destined to be an accountant. In my last few months in Washington, Justin Bereny and I took the CPA exam. It was kind of on a whim. We just enrolled for the exam without taking a review course. We studied a little, but really just figured we had nothing to lose, and an experience to gain. I passed two of the three parts at that time, and then intended to take the last part after I got out of the service. Some months later I did take it, and passed.

I spent a year or two trying to help my dad's business, but I also quickly realized I had to follow my own path. At age 27 I decided that if I was ever going to get started in public accounting, now was the time.

I remember well the meeting in which I told my father I was moving on. He was, of course, disappointed. I don't know that I would use the word upset. It wasn't like I was walking out on some thriving venture that would collapse without me. But I'm sure he hoped I would stay to share the growth and experience.

I told him my younger brother might be available after finishing his army stint. Without wanting to speak for Joel, I felt he might be more interested in this type of a business. As it turned out, I was right for myself, my brother and my father.

The business continued to improve and got even better when Joel came along. My father was a great salesman. He didn't know how to take no for an answer if he believed in what he was selling. But he wasn't really organized and didn't run things terribly well. Joel ended up running the business while my father took more time looking after the needs of the employees he had come to know so well. They were a perfect team, and some 40 years later the business stands as a great legacy to my father's dreams.

My dad died of cancer in 1984. At his funeral, I wrote and read a eulogy that included the same poetic passages that Rabbi Ralph Simon read at my Great-Aunt Etta's funeral 10 years earlier. It also included a few thoughts on my father's life and legacy. The following is an excerpt from that eulogy.

■ ■ ■

> Greatness is hard to define or measure, but in my mind, because my father cared about people, and acted on his beliefs, he was truly a great man.
>
> He obviously loved his family and showed it in his givings of all kinds — to his grandchildren, their typewriters, books and affection; to Ellen and Lenore, the knowledge that they were truly "his" daughters; to all of us, being there whenever needed "quality time," as they now like to call it.
>
> One thing I remember vividly was when he and Joel and I played basketball in the bedroom using a wire hanger bent over the door with a pair of rolled up socks. He would shoot free throws underhand like Rick Barry, and as good as Joel and I were, he almost always won.

My mother was a great comfort and source of strength to him, not always in ways obvious. They went everywhere together, all the more so in later years. Be it plays, concerts, the Cubs, life was to be lived and he did so to the end.

... He loved his co-workers and I hope and think he knew they loved him back. He also loved his monthly poker club, and since cards were not one of his strengths, they loved him back doubly.

... He could be stubborn, tough, rigid, he had trouble compromising even when basic principles might not have been involved. Whether with the American Jewish Congress, Voters for Peace, Free Mass Transportation, Russia & China Friendship Councils, Civil Rights & Liberties, Nuclear Freeze or in his personal life, the interests of people and their survival were always paramount to him....

■ ■ ■

I was proud of those words then. Now, as I reflect on the true impact he had on my life, I am even prouder.

CHAPTER V
A Partner and Husband

My search for a position in the accounting field began and ended in the *Chicago Tribune*. I answered an ad for a junior accountant and later met with Jerry Harris from the firm of Shepard, Schwartz & Harris. He hired me, and I started what's now been a 40-year career in accounting. Jerry and I still have lunch once a month and discuss the state of the world, of politics and of our accounting practices. A couple of months ago Jerry said, "Harvey, it's time for you to stop worrying about things." When I asked him why, he said, "Because you don't have that many years left for things to go wrong."

After being hired, I moved into an apartment in Chicago at the Park Royal in Lincoln Park. I was smart enough to know I'd need a building that supplied maid service and had a late night restaurant inside. I can remember many nights getting home at about 11 p.m. and the little restaurant was waiting for me.

Shepard, Schwartz & Harris was probably a 30-person firm at the time. This was in the days when people didn't really use computers, everything was done by hand and done mathematically. Young people were checking older people's work for addition errors or writing errors. In those days, however, the laws were not nearly as complicated and didn't have all these partnership questions and passive losses and carry-forwards and a million other things we have today.

The computer, of course, has greatly helped all accountants, as well as almost every other profession. The excitement of working with new technology is exhilarating in many ways. I even learned DOS last year, and Windows this year.

Irv Shepard and Morrie Schwartz were the other two partners, and founders, of the firm. Irv was an entrepreneurial sort with a number of investments in real estate. For some reason at the end of every year he would call me into his office and show me how much his net worth had increased that year. I had a little trouble understanding the point of this exercise. He would show me what he was worth at the beginning of the year and then the end of the year. Whatever the numbers, it was a lot of money. As I got older I realized this was one of the ways we as people tend to measure ourselves. It proves, I guess, that we're still vital, active and productive. That's how I took it anyway.

One of the first jobs I had at the firm was auditing the Hotel Corporation of Israel, which was actually the Sheraton Tel-Aviv Hotel. To a great extent the hotel was built on Israeli bond money, which I wasn't terribly experienced in. As I got into it, though, I figured it out. But that doesn't mean there weren't some adventures.

A couple of years later, in the middle of tax season, I went over to the hotel's office to count the Israeli bonds. I'll never forget they were supposed to have about $880,000 worth of Israeli bonds in order for everything to balance, and they only had about $800,000.

Because Irv was the partner in charge, I went in to tell him about this problem. I didn't know yet that Irv had a habit of laughing when he got a little nervous, so when he started laughing at the situation I began to lose it myself. But I wasn't laughing.

Now, I had been employed there awhile and at that point was working harder than I should have been, harder than anybody should have been. I was still single, and spent most of my time at the office. All of the partners at that firm were in their mid to late 30s when they got married. Whether that is a character trait of the business or coincidental is a good question. I am not and never will be the kind of person who tells anybody that we worked harder in the old days, because everyone who wants to get anywhere is working hard.

Anyway, Shepard started laughing as if it was entirely my fault that they were short Israeli bonds. Although I should have been a bit more diplomatic, I told him I couldn't go on this way. I told him I was killing myself at this job, that I'd been doing taxes from 7 to 11 at night, after an audit work day that started at seven in the morning. I needed some help, I said, and it wasn't my fault that they came up short on the bonds.

The bottom line is, I went a little too far. Jerry Harris called me in the next day and said, right or wrong, you can't talk to a senior partner that way. Of course, he was right. I should have gone through channels. But some weeks later

Jerry told me that, ironically, he was on the receiving end of a similar situation at about the same point in his career and did the same thing. But he made sure to say, don't do it again. Just recently, Jerry's partners threw him a gala party celebrating his 75th birthday and his 50 years with the firm. Ellen and I were there and were thrilled to see such a great tribute to a man who truly deserved it.

While Irv Shepard was more of the promoter type, Morrie Schwartz had come by way of Arthur Andersen. When he passed the CPA exam he received a silver medal for ranking second in the state. That's amazing. He was a very smart, very thorough and very private person — and an outstanding bridge player.

I got along very well with Morrie, and I remember him walking up to me on a Friday at about 5 p.m. and asking me if I had any plans for the night. Not anymore, I said. We both laughed, but that's the attitude I had. If something needed to be done, I'd usually had no qualms about staying as long as it took.

I remember seriously considering getting a masters in taxation at New York University, one of the few universities in the country offering such a program. Morrie said to me, you can do that, but it won't help you in a practice such as ours, and it certainly won't help teach you how to deal with revenue agents. He was right, and I didn't pursue it.

I do feel I've really learned how to deal with revenue agents, however. As you may know, tax audits can come in one of three ways: by a random computer selection, by an issue on a tax return that jumps out at a reviewer (either because of its nature or dollar amount) or because of a mismatch of forms, such as W-2, 1099, etc.

The first cause of an audit has greatly diminished over the

years. Without getting political, during Ronald Reagan's presidency he dramatically reduced the number of IRS agents in a cost-cutting move. To me that never made much sense because it would be like firing your top salesmen. In any case, it did result in significantly fewer office and field audits. Last year there were 200 million returns filed and only two million audits, obviously only 1%. It should be noted that about 83% of individuals voluntarily pay their full tax bill — a rate that has remained steady for two decades and is probably the highest in the world.

Regarding the second cause of an audit, some years ago a revenue ruling was promulgated, which in effect put a great burden on tax preparers where there were "questionable" issues involved. My personal theory has always been to take the most aggressive approach consistent with my basic principles — with the litmus test being which side would I rather argue if I had to go to court. So, on a debatable issue, this new regulation requires us to disclose it on the return, in a sense making us part of the government team. Because of something like that, or just because of unusual items, the second audit can arise.

Finally, under the 1986 Tax Reform Act, almost all trusts, partnerships and 'S' corporations had to adopt a calendar year for reporting. Besides causing additional tax-season anguish for all of us, it allowed the government to get payors and payees on the same reporting period, thereby expediting their computer monitoring program. Many notices that taxpayers receive are a direct result of this action.

Most issues get resolved at the audit level, but if agreement cannot be reached, an appeal process is available. If that doesn't work for you, the last step is tax court, where you have to pay the assessed tax and then sue for a refund. You do not want to go to tax court — I've never had to.

So, as I said, I've had really good luck working with agents. Without meaning to boast, I honestly don't feel there's been even one matter in 40 years for which I did not get eventual basic satisfaction for my client. People do not like to get IRS notices, for obvious reasons, but when they do I see it as my job to tell them they shouldn't worry, and then go out and prove it.

My theory is that in spite of much recent negative publicity, IRS agents are not really as bad as they're portrayed. Of course, it would be absurd to believe there aren't abuses. But I do not believe, for instance, that the White House put the IRS on Paula Jones, although some over-exuberant agent may clearly have gotten carried away.

Agents have a lot of restrictions put on them, so I try to be friendly, ask how they are doing, ask about family pictures on their desk, etc. That doesn't stop me from being tough but decent. I also take every opportunity to teach agents something about the tax laws, and they almost always appreciate it. Because clients may say more than they need to, which can raise questions that don't need to be asked, I try to go alone

Of the many IRS stories I've experienced over the years, two remain my favorites. In the "old" days you didn't necessarily know who the agent would be until you got there. One day I was in the IRS office talking to a receptionist I had gotten to know while waiting for an agent. When the agent emerged, the receptionist shook her head negatively, which I took to mean, you've got trouble. She was right. After almost an hour of procedural questions, which should normally take a matter of minutes, I told the agent this just isn't going to work. I asked to see his supervisor to request a change of auditors, which you can do once in each case. The agent told me he didn't think his supervisor was in. I told him to please try anyway. So he picks up his phone and hits a few numbers. The phone on the empty desk next to us begins to ring. I said, are you calling that number? He said yes, I told you I didn't think she was in.

The second experience was a little different. We had an agent who had absolutely no clue and was 100% wrong on a major corporate issue. His supervisor said he understood our position, but for his own reasons couldn't overrule the agent (it may have had something to do with not overruling new agents). In any case, I drafted and sent an appeals brief, walked in a month later and the appeals officer looked at me and said, "This is absurd. You're absolutely right. Go home." They should all be so easy.

All in all, I think I'm a pretty good accountant. But a lot of people whom I've worked with over the years, and am working with now, are probably better at certain technical aspects of it than I. I think my greatest asset over the years has been my judgment. I also tend to like people, and I think they like me. That's more important than it may sound. Building relationships and caring about people has been as integral to my success as managing numbers. I've always thought of myself as a financial therapist.

While my relationships have been nurtured over a number of years, many of them have had to overcome a personality that doesn't always transmit well over the phone. Many people have chided me for my curt manner on the phone, and I've told them not to take it personally. My daughters continue to kid me about it, telling me the impression they get from talking to me on the phone is not always one of the loving father I am.

I owe my quick phone fashion, I think, to the sense of

impatience I've had all my life. I say what I have to say and get on with things. I'm a bit compulsive about returning calls. You may not always reach me, but I always return calls in a timely manner. I was especially brief when I first went off on my own. There were just too many things to be done to justify hanging on the phone for long, but I believe I've gotten a lot better over the years.

I had a number of accounts at Shepard, Schwartz & Harris that I'll never forget. Not every one brought with it a great experience, but in my years there I met a number of tremendous characters and was lucky to have learned quite a bit about this city, and about life.

One of my biggest accounts was Leaf Brands, the candy and gum company. Unfortunately, their year-end was January 31, which meant their corporate tax return was due April 15 — along with everything else in the world that was due April 15.

I remember the audits I did at company headquarters. Sol Leaf was the founder and patriarch of the family, but spent the winters in Palm Springs. By then his sons and his nephew, Leslie Shankman, were running the business. Sol had a beautiful paneled office with absolutely no windows. I could never understand that. I would get there at seven in the morning and spend all day in this cave-like office, and I remember saying to myself either there ought to be some windows in this building or I ought to be in a different business.

These types of trips took me from Wisconsin to Indiana. One client was Henry Stein, the man who founded the Steinway Drugstore chain. He was getting older, but was not quite the type to retire, so he worked out of a drugstore on Roger Williams Avenue in Highland Park, a northern suburb about 20 miles from the city.

I used to go up there every two to three months, and I remember wondering why anyone would want to live this far out. I guess you see things differently as you grow older, because I now live just three miles from that drugstore. Fortunately, the train system in the northern suburbs of Chicago matches any transit system in the world, which makes the suburbs that much closer. But in those days living on the North Shore seemed like something I would never do.

Another client of mine sat on the other end of the area, in East Chicago, Indiana. It was actually two men who were in the insurance and real estate business. One was Greek and an all-time, all-American drinker. I remember going down there periodically, and every afternoon around three he'd say let's have a drink, and I'd say, no, I have to work, and I have to drive. He looked at me one day and said I just can't do this anymore, I'm not going to drink before five o'clock. I said, that sounds like a good idea to me, and I left.

I arrived at his office the next day at 9 a.m. and there he was, drinking. I looked at him and said, I thought you weren't going to drink before five o'clock. He smiled and said, "Harvey, it's five o'clock somewhere."

Of all my early accounts, however, the most significant one was a real estate and shopping center development firm called Landau & Heyman. Howard Landau and Herb Heyman were two of the finest gentlemen I had ever known. I later came to learn we shared the same political and social consciousness views, but it all started with the accounting.

The attorney representing Landau & Heyman was a man named Howard Kane. Kane was with Jenner & Block at the time and is still one of the top real estate lawyers in Chicago at Rudnick & Wolfe. In our dealings, we spent some time talking about both business and social matters and came to know each other pretty well. He told me about a lady named Lynne Walker Goldblatt who was getting divorced from Joel Goldblatt, one of the Goldblatt brothers of the famous Goldblatt department store chain.

Howard Kane had such a fine reputation for fairness, intelligence and integrity that both parties of the divorce agreed to work with Howard toward reaching an amicable understanding. Once they were divorced, Howard told me Lynne had been financially watched over during her marriage and would now need an accountant. He told me someone had to help her get on and stay on an even keel.

When I became Lynne's accountant, I had no idea I'd soon gain another impressive client and a wonderful friend. She married Leo Durocher just a few years later.

Anyway, I'm 30 years old when I get called into the office where the three accounting partners sit. They ask me if I'd like to be a partner. Sure, I'd like to be a partner. That's what I had been building toward and looking forward to. They said good. It was practically that simple.

In 1960, I clearly remember I was making $12,000 a year as the firm's top staff person. After all parties agreed I would be the fourth partner in the firm, Jerry Harris said, just so you know, you'll have to take a pay cut to $11,200 because you have to buy into the capital of the firm. I was kind of on a high and I suppose as long as he left me enough to live on, I would have agreed to anything.

This was 37 years ago, and I don't know what $11,000 would be worth today, but those were the salaries then. When I was a kid growing up I once thought, like all of us, if I ever made $5,000 a year, that would be enough, that would put me in the top 1% of the world. So much for inflation.

I was a partner for another couple of years, and it was a

very pleasant experience. I still worked awfully hard, but I liked everybody. I remember being told that sometimes the partners get investment opportunities, and that I'd get a chance to be a part of it to the extent that I could afford to invest. I don't know if that was a significant offer on their part because they knew I couldn't afford to invest, but the idea of having an opportunity to get something going beyond my hard, day-to-day efforts was, of course, appealing to me.

Unfortunately, the first time some investment came along on an account that I was working on, no one told me about it. There was an investment opportunity through Ronnie Benach and Stu Grill who started 3H Homes out in Hanover Park. They have since become extremely successful men. Everyone who invested with them has done extremely well, and there was a partnership formed from it. But no one even mentioned the opportunity to me, let alone gave me the chance to invest in it. That didn't set too well with me because a promise is a promise and, for better or worse, I should have been given an opportunity. I never knew why I wasn't.

Another one of my long-distance clients was in Harvey, Illinois. I used to go there to do the audit. It was after returning from a trip there that I was first introduced, so to speak, to the woman who would become my wife.

A tennis buddy of mine named Bob Paley and a good friend, Bob Sugarman, called me, not to set up a tennis game, but to set up a meeting with this woman they said I'd really like. Both Bobs had girlfriends (whom they eventually married) and they, and this young woman, were all together for the evening. I told Bob Paley how tired I was and that I was looking forward to a nice, long sleep in my own bed. With all his badgering I said, "Why don't you just let me talk to this girl on the phone, and maybe we can get together later on."

Well, she didn't want to talk on the phone. If someone wanted to meet her, they could do it in person or not at all — at least that was the message I got from the decline.

This woman, I learned, had been teaching in California for a couple of years and had just returned to Chicago. Her father was the owner of a boys' camp in Wisconsin, and she intrigued me a bit. I dragged myself out that night and met Ellen. We hit it off, and three or four months later we were married.

I remember telling her we can get married toward the end of December, but we can't go on a honeymoon because I have to start tax season. She had no problem with that.

I was a partner in an accounting firm, and my new wife was teaching at a nearby school. Life was good and moving on. Still, I was getting restless.

Much to my surprise, the first client that I ever brought in to the firm was turning out to be the most demanding. I met Frank Fried at a political rally. I went to the event to hear someone speak and Frank and I started talking. He said I've heard about you and I haven't filed any tax returns for three or four years. He said, I don't like my present accountant and I'd like to talk to you.

A few years later I was doing a tremendous amount of work for Frank — I was literally running the financial aspects of his companies — and he began encouraging me to join him exclusively. Frank's Triangle Productions was the popular concert promoter in Chicago and the Midwest. In those days he booked all the rock groups, including the Beatles and the Rolling Stones as well as Frank Sinatra, Barbra Streisand, Peter, Paul and Mary and others. You name it, and he did it.

One of the groups Frank brought in was the Chad Mitchell Trio, which at the time was right up there with Peter,

Paul and Mary and the Kingston Trio. He and Chad Mitchell became partners in both Triangle Productions and the Chad Mitchell Trio, which was comprised of Chad, Mike Kobluk and Joe Frazier. They also ran a production company, a publishing company and a recording company, where I was spending a lot of my time. They didn't want anybody but me, so I had to do it, and eventually they reached a point where they asked me to join them as the third equal owner of Triangle and the Trio.

Of course, this was all very enticing for a young man like me. This was a progressive singing group, and even though I was smart enough to realize this was not a long-term answer, I certainly entertained the thought.

I went to Jerry Harris, who by that time had become a great friend. I told him about the offer and that it was a difficult one for me to turn down. I also confided in him that I didn't think there was any long-term stability there, so I asked him what he thought of the possibility of the firm becoming the partner instead of me, or through me. I would hold a degree of ownership through them, and would just work with Frank for awhile to help that business reach its potential. But I would still be a partner at the accounting firm, I would be considered on loan or on assignment for some time.

Either Jerry thought it was a good idea or he didn't want to lose me, or both, because he said he thought we could work something like that out. Frank and Chad, however, didn't like that approach. They didn't want me having any dual loyalties, so they said it was one way or the other. I did not leave the firm because I recognized the inherent risk and fragility of the move.

Another year or so went by and the frustration of handling

more audits clashed with the continual work load coming from Frank and Chad.

So, I decided to leave public accounting and take a shot at this venture of Fried's. At that time, Ellen and I had had our first daughter, Susan, and were living in an apartment near Lake Shore Drive.

In looking back, that was a gutsy decision, but it seemed to make sense to me at the time. With some misgivings and a lot of trepidation, I told Jerry that I was ready to move on. He couldn't talk me out of it, and the next saga of my life was about to begin.

CHAPTER VI
Some Entertaining Options

I wasn't totally naive about the risk involved in making this kind of career move. I realized working with Frank Fried wasn't a ticket to long-term stability. Chad Mitchell, a performer in the entertainment field, was obviously only committed for as long as he was willing to go on. I guess it was the excitement and the feeling of getting a leg up on life that enticed me to join Triangle Productions. So I did.

As I said, they were the biggest concert promoters in the Midwest. That made for some exciting times. I used to go to Frank's apartment after work and it was always a real party. This was when folk music was at its peak. Bob Gibson and Joe Mapes were the big names in Chicago, and they'd play around town and then show up at Frank's along with some other well-known names. There was always something going on.

The Chad Mitchell Trio was also one of the big acts, and their music seemed to flow with the politics of the time. The civil rights movement was taking hold, and you could find the day's headlines weaved into the songs that Chad, Mike and Joe were singing. It was a truly enlightening time.

Chad Mitchell's story is an interesting one. Some time before I ever met him, he appeared on *The Ed Sullivan Show* as one of three future singing stars of the decade. The other two were Barbra Streisand and Georgia Brown. Ironically, the late John Denver got his first big break when he eventually replaced Chad Mitchell.

Chad had one of those great voices that went well with his very boyish on-stage charm. I believe he met his partners, Joe and Mike, at Gonzaga College in the state of Washington, where they first began singing together.

They were pretty big, pretty quick. Their concerts were always sell-outs. One night toward the end of their career Frank booked the band into the Camellia House of the Drake Hotel. Ironically, that's where Ellen and I had our wedding dinner. It was a pretty fancy place, and it seemed kind of incongruous to me that the Chad Mitchell Trio would perform there.

As it turned out, my premonitions were correct. The Pepsi-Cola Corporation had coincidentally booked some sort of convention in the Drake that same week. Many of their executives, including the top ones, were in the Camellia House for dinner and the show one night. I don't think the Pepsi-Cola people had the slightest idea who the Chad Mitchell Trio was or, if they did, they didn't seem to care. The band started their routine, with a lot of progressive songs that included one about "Old Miss" and the state's attempts to keep blacks out of school. One of the executives, who happened to be sitting at the table right next to a group I was with, threw a penny on the floor and said, "Go buy yourself an education." I'm sure he had had too much to drink.

When Joe Frazier, who was the most radical member of the Trio, heard that, he stopped the show, picked up the penny, walked over to the man's table, dropped the penny in front of the man who threw it and said, "Here, take this, you need it a lot more than I do."

That, as you may or may not have guessed, set off a mini-riot. The Pepsi-Cola executive took a wine bottle, broke it off at the neck and started after Joe. I don't consider myself any great hero, but that situation got the best of me. I grabbed the bottle-wielding executive from behind, locked his arms in mine and pinned him to the side until others could help disarm him.

We all ended up at the police station that night. I think some charges were pressed and probably some kind of settlement made, but nothing too significant ever came of it.

My wife and I remember well the first year of our marriage because we spent almost every Saturday night at McCormick Place or some other concert hall. I had to be at the concerts because I had to balance everything out, and pay off the entertainers. We usually paid the entertainers half of their money in advance and the rest the night of the event. One night, Woody Allen went on, did his routine and at intermission came up to me and asked where the other half of his check was. I told him he was supposed to have gotten it from someone in our office. He said he'd gotten nothing, and that he wasn't going back on until he got the rest of his pay. Things obviously got a little tense really quickly. We rushed around and, of course, got him paid without any more fuss.

Other than a few missteps like that, the business seemed

to be moving along smoothly. There was another promoter in town named Harry Zelzer. He was the classical promoter, bringing in all the concerts and ballets. His specialty at that time was bringing in the famous Russian dancers, but he was just as famous for what he'd say about audiences. He said, "If they want to come, you can't stop them. And if they don't want to come, you can't stop them." I definitely found that to be true.

I remember we used to agonize over whether to charge $3.50 or $3.75 for a concert ticket. In hindsight it's like everything else on pricing. If people want it, they'll pay for it. If they don't want it, there really isn't a price that's likely to attract them.

When our first daughter, Susan, was born, it seemed as though we had cleared the hurdles and made my career change worthwhile. Then, as all good things come to an end, Chad Mitchell came over to our apartment for dinner one night and dropped the bomb. He couldn't go on anymore. He said the three of them, the Trio, weren't getting along well. He needed to break it up.

I told Chad I would have appreciated it if he'd mentioned this possibility to me before I made my big move, but at that point, there wasn't much I could do about it. The boys struggled on for awhile, but the writing was in the sands. Chad moved on, and John Denver filled in for awhile before the band faded away.

Chad tried a solo career for a time, but was just never comfortable on his own. He is now a cruise director for the Delta Queen.

This break-up, of course, affected everything, including Frank's attitude. To me, he seemed to get more difficult to deal with. I realized my adventure was about to come to an end. After a short period of reflection, I decided I'd better fend for myself.

Harry Zelzer had started a ticket service in Chicago. Well, he hadn't started it, but he was using the Sears stores to distribute tickets for his classical concerts and events. This operation was the forerunner to the ticket service now known as Ticketmaster. At that time, however, you would just call the Sears stores or go in to a store and reserve tickets with a charge card or your Sears card. A small service charge was added and then you'd pick them up under your name the night of the concert. These tickets, however, were limited to the concerts Zelzer produced.

I began looking into this idea and realized there might be a bigger and better way of doing it. There was a major service similar to this operating in Los Angeles, which I visited. It wasn't a broker, it was a service to the public.

Although Zelzer's idea was sound, I was convinced it wasn't operating quite right. People were unhappy, and it wasn't paying off for anybody.

I went to Sears and told them I could do this for them and include all the events in the city, run it more efficiently and bring in more profit. Sears turned me down, said they weren't interested in doing that. They were content going on in their own limited way.

One of the agreements I had with Frank Fried when I left Triangle Productions was that if I could get this ticket service project off the ground, I could handle all of his tickets. After my rejection from Sears I went to Montgomery Ward, which had a lot of stores in the city and suburbs. I told them my plan and they were anxious to do it because Sears was doing it.

We got off to a great start with Montgomery Ward, but it soon became obvious Sears was not happy with the inroads we were making. They went to all of our potential customers and, in effect, said, we'll now do this for nothing. Their hope was to put us out of business before we grew wings.

I called Howard Kane and told him I needed an antitrust lawyer, and he called a man named Phil Tone, who eventually became a judge.

With one phone call from Tone, basically saying, "Do you want antitrust publicity and litigation over Harvey Wineberg?" Sears had a change in corporate policy overnight, and I was in business. I found a record store on Michigan Avenue just south of the river. It had a balcony that wasn't being used very advantageously and an office on the lower level. They were looking for traffic, so I started Ticket Central.

Over the course of a year or two I visited everybody in the city — all the theater and concert and sporting event types — and got as many customers for Ticket Central as I could. I didn't visit Harry Zelzer, who stayed with Sears and never did do it right.

We got into ticket sales at the height of the popular concert game. We'd have thousands of people using our service for one night. The lines would be very long, but we got it all done.

Ironically, the only person other than Zelzer that I could not get as a customer was Arthur Wirtz, owner of the Chicago Blackhawks and the Chicago Stadium. I went up to his office once to talk. We sat there and had lunch. The lunch was pleasant enough, but he was as difficult a man as I've ever known.

I did, however, get a lesson in the Wirtz business philosophy. During that meeting he asked me what I thought it was worth to him financially to have just raised the price of beer at the stadium from 50 to 75 cents. I asked if he was talking about all events or just the Bulls and the Blackhawks. All events, he said. We get everything. I said I have no way of knowing, but how about a half-million dollars? He looked at me somewhat respectfully and said that's a very, very good guess. I said, yes, but you're presuming that consumption will stay at its present level. After all, you are raising the price 50%, and you can't count on having the demand that you had before. He looked at me haughtily and said, there are no water fountains in the stadium. What else are they going to drink?

Well, Wirtz didn't sign a contract, but did eventually use us. Ticket Central became a moderately successful venture. That, combined with the re-creation of my own personal service accounting practice, kept me awfully busy. One-by-one people I knew or knew of began to come to me for accounting and tax services. I was sitting there in my little office doing accounting and running Ticket Central, and upstairs my unionized box office men were working away under the direction of Bobby Hoffman.

Bob Hoffman is now a close friend and has been head of the ticket sellers union for a number of years. He used to be a "red neck," but has really grown over the years into an enlightened business manager. He and Butch Wonder are the two main box office men at the United Center, which is the successor to the Chicago Stadium. In those days, we ended up working with almost every box office in the city.

Again, I was juggling a lot of things when my second daughter, Julie, was born. I was trying to figure out how to make some real progress in this world when I got a call from a man named Jack Quinn in New York. Quinn had been hired by the Bronfman family, who own Seagram's. Quinn told me they want to start a computerized ticket distribution system in the country, would I be interested in talking to them? I had nothing to lose, so of course I wanted to talk.

Quinn came to Chicago to meet and the next thing I knew I was handling Chicago and the Midwest for this new, nationwide ticket service called Ticket Reservation Systems, which later became Ticketron and, finally, Ticket Master. This new job involved overseeing the system throughout the Midwest, which led to some traveling to help other cities start up. It was a very exciting position.

I got the chance to talk with Edgar Bronfman, the head of Seagram's in New York. He said to me, you seem to be the only person who knows what they're doing. The others were all computer people and systems people. I was the only one who had any real experience in the financial, entertainment and sports fields. Bronfman asked me how long I thought it would take to break even. Money certainly wasn't a worry to him, but nobody goes into business to lose money. I looked at him and said, "I don't know, but I would guess four years and $40 million."

That long? he wondered. I don't think this has huge money-making potential, I told him. What's going to make money in this whole approach is the state gambling lotteries, and if you want to get into that, that's probably where the company belongs.

The company lost money year after year. Control Data Corporation became the hardware supplier for the various systems. We had computers in four or five cities throughout the country and, of course, terminals hooked up to them everywhere. All the box offices in Chicago were computerized as a result of these efforts. I'm not sure everybody appreciated what I was doing because it was a big change for all of them, but I think they now realize it was inevitable. We moved over to Marina City, where we had the computer center for the whole Midwest online system.

Meanwhile, I was practicing accounting while running a company. Somehow I would get the tax returns and statements out. I had one secretary to help me, everybody else worked for Ticketron. Sure enough, after about four years, Bronfman decided he had had enough. He lost the $40 million I talked about, but he wasn't breaking even, so he sold out to Control Data because they were interested in keeping the market for their hardware.

I received some stock in Ticketron at the beginning, so when Control Data eventually bought everyone out, including me, it gave me enough to upgrade the co-op apartment Ellen and I had bought on Lake Shore Drive.

We got this great apartment on the 14th floor, which we loved, although I have no idea why I thought I could afford it. Sometimes what we don't know doesn't hurt us.

Not long after the move, our third daughter, Margi, was born. Although I had been bought out, I was still with Ticketron under a five-year contract for Control Data, and life was all right.

One of my not-so-favorite things was the chaotic work life of running the Ticketron business with my box office friends upstairs, and practicing accounting downstairs with my trusted secretary, Margaret McCombs. Margaret and I had worked together since our days at Triangle. I had great respect for her.

As much as the excitement still got to me and the idea was still fresh, I knew enough about the entertainment industry to know that Ticketron was not where I would spend the rest of my career. I knew I would be voluntarily out as soon as my five-year contract with Ticketron was up. I also knew I wasn't the type to work for a big company. I wasn't likely to work for anyone but myself. While that's a liberating observation, it's also one that comes with its share of pressure. Pressure or not, I realized it was time to devote myself to really developing my accounting practice.

When my fourth daughter, Nancy, was born, our obstetrician told the nurse that he never comes out to tell a father he's had the fourth of any sex, so he sent the nurse out to tell me.

Although I would have loved to have a son, Dr. Lawrence Bernard had no need to be concerned. I cannot conceive (pun intended) of having had a son in place of any of my four daughters. They have each kidded me over the years with, "I'm your favorite, right?" And with each I've answered yes. They are very smart, but I think it took them some time to realize that I answer them all that way because they are all my favorites.

With four daughters, I knew I had at least four college tuitions ahead of me. What I was shooting for was to live a balanced life that would enable me to do what I wanted to do while providing for my family.

With the exception of Ticketron and Frank Fried's Triangle Promotions, Jerry and Betty Abeles were my first clients. We had been friends for quite awhile and I appreciated their confidence in me then, and I appreciate it even more now. We've had a lot of good years together, and it's nice to see how relationships can mature to the point where everything turned out as we hoped.

I remember being very busy one April 13 in particular. It was late when I got a call from a resident surgeon who had just moved into town from Pennsylvania. This Dr. Leonard Cerullo said someone gave him my name, and that he needed his tax return done.

I was about to tell him how you can't call me on April 13

and expect to get your tax return done in 48 hours. Fortunately, my better judgment prevailed. I said, sure, I guess we can do that. That began a long-term friendship with the brain surgeon and laser pioneer that is stronger than either of us could have imagined. Not only is he considered one of the best neurosurgeons in the world, but he is a very warm, very smart man. He loves people and they love him back. He always seems to know exactly what it is that people need. We talk at least once a day and though it may seem unusual, we both think everything we say is important. His wife, Cheryl, is also a good friend of ours.

I take a lot of pride in being somewhat responsible for his move from his original post at Northwestern Hospital to Columbus Hospital. I not only encouraged the move, but helped negotiate it. At Columbus, he set up a Neurosurgical Center for Excellency that now involves 15 other neurosurgeons. He and his business associate, Peter Breen, are now doing some very exciting things in medicine. They just formed a new company called NeuroSource, which manages neurosurgical practices all over the country and promises to be the way of future health care. I'm proud to be on the board of that company with them.

Life really takes strange turns. Peter Breen is the son of Leo Breen, who, when I was negotiating contracts for both Bill Melton and Ken Henderson of the Chicago White Sox, was the top gun at the White Sox. Leo Breen, by everyone's recollection and knowledge, was one of the really true gentlemen and smart people in professional sports, and I always get a kick out of it when I look at Peter and remember his father. I say this, not because Peter is now a good friend of mine, but because it's absolutely true.

By this time, my practice was well off the ground and

Ellen had stopped teaching school to take a full-time job raising four daughters. She is absolutely the best. They don't make mothers like her anymore. She was born to be a mother. She knows how to raise children, when to be tough, when to be funny and when to be nurturing. I just can't imagine a better mother.

Our major problem living in the apartment was the close quarters. It was a bit confining. It also got a little tough taking four children, ranging from age six to less than a year, out to play when you had to wait for the elevator and worry about the problems of the city. When the oldest, Susan, was ready to go to grammar school, we took her to the neighborhood public school and, at least, had serious thoughts about trying to make all of this work.

There was a new magnet school about two blocks away from us, but we found out there was no preference for siblings. Chances were, if you had one child in, you wouldn't be able to get others in. So, we ended up trying the public school. The principal at that school said it's too long a walk from your house to this school, and suggested we not consider it. I countered that something could be worked out. She said, what if I told you the school was 70% transient and that I didn't think your kids would be best-served by being here? Whether she was right or not, that's the sad plight of the Chicago Public School System.

The most serious problem in our country, and particularly this city, is the education system. I get the feeling we're finally trying to do at least more about it than we have in the past. In my particular case, I just couldn't see that working out, and I certainly couldn't see paying to send four children to private school.

So, in 1970, we did what for me was somewhat traumatic

and, for a while, unthinkable. We moved out to the northern suburbs in a day from hell. Picture four children aged six and under on a freezing and windy February day. The movers came at 7 a.m. and left at midnight. The weather was so bad, they could hardly get up the driveway.

Not only did we move to the northern suburbs, we moved pretty far north to Highland Park, about 25 miles north of downtown Chicago. I remember telling Ellen the only condition I had was to be close enough to walk to the train. We were lucky enough to find this unbelievable English Tudor house that sat on three-quarters of an acre and was two blocks from the Ravinia Festival — a home I don't think I ever dreamed I would live in. Sure, plenty of things needed fixing, but we got through it despite the fact that I don't think I was a very good financial advisor to myself at that time. The theory is, if you stay healthy and keep working, somehow you will solve your problems.

Leaving the city wasn't easy for me. Sure, I'd miss the bustling excitement of living in the thick of things, but what also concerned me was my increasing distance from Wrigley Field. A faithful fan of the Chicago Cubs, I wasn't sure how this move would affect my ability to drop in on a game every now and then. Before we left, however, something very special happened. Like everyone else I had finally had enough of the team's dismal record and parade of hopeless coaches. I told some friends that if they'd only bring in a firebrand manager like Leo Durocher, maybe this would all turn around and Cub fans would have at least a chance to have a winner.

In the late 1960s, much to my pleasant surprise, the Wrigley family decided to hire Leo Durocher as manager. Leo was already a legend as a player and as a manager. This decision was a blessing for the team and for the city. It also turned out to be a blessing for me.

I was still representing Lynne Walker Goldblatt, who by then had gotten to know Leo well. Eventually, I met Leo through Lynne.

I only knew Leo casually when he told me he liked me. He said, "I think you're smart and honest, but I've never had any business manager or accountant who hasn't tried to take advantage of me. I don't trust anybody," he said. I told him that was just fine, that he wasn't compelled to do any business with me.

Not too long after that, Leo came to me again. He said, "I think you should handle all my financial affairs." I did, until the day he died.

CHAPTER VII
Leo the Lip

Any true fan of the Chicago Cubs who was around in 1969 can probably still feel the pain of that disastrous season. I know I can. I remember clearly the turn of events that saw the Cubs lose a commanding lead in the standings to the New York Mets in the last month of the season. Leo was managing the team, and had done a great job. But, as is known all too well, the Mets went on an unbelievable winning streak, caught the Cubs and went on to win the World Series.

As a fan, that was really an emotionally draining time, a frustrating disappointment. It was tough for Leo, who was one of the most competitive men I've ever known, but he was also a professional who could deal with losing. He had a saying that I still try to live by today. When someone would ask him how he did, he would never say, we lost. He'd always say, we got beat.

By the time I met Leo, in the mid-1960s, he had become more of a private person than he was during his early life. He was still a large personality, a charming curmudgeon and a great leader of men. He was also a good friend to Frank Sinatra. But Leo seemed most comfortable among small groups of friends. He didn't necessarily shun the public, but he didn't pursue attention either.

Shortly after I met Leo, he and Lynne Walker Goldblatt married. Lynne was Leo's third wife. Long before I knew him he had been married to Lorraine Day, the movie actress. I met her at Leo's funeral. Before Lorraine, Leo had married a clothes designer in St. Louis.

One winter Ellen and I joined Leo and Lynne, along with Joey Amalfitano and his girlfriend on a trip to Acapulco. Amalfitano was Leo's long-time friend and fellow baseball coach. Wherever Leo went to manage, Amalfitano seemed to follow. He's been coaching the Los Angeles Dodgers now for years.

Leo was one of those people who insisted you do it his way or you don't do it. He rented a mansion for the trip, a gorgeous place with plenty of bedrooms, lots of help, a pool, the works. On one of the first nights there Leo told me I needed some Mexican-type clothes. I told him I have clothes, but he insisted I didn't — not the right kind, anyway. He dragged me into a tailor shop and bought me three outfits that I wore all week, and probably never wore again.

That's how he was. He had a fetish for clothes. He'd line up his shirts and slacks in his closet by color, from light to dark. He probably had fifteen identical shirts and slacks. But he always looked very dapper.

To the world, Leo always seemed to be well off financially, despite the fact that he played and managed in an era when big money contracts did not exist. He always seemed to have enough for what he wanted to do.

One day at Wrigley Field, someone asked him if he'd make an appearance somewhere for $500. Leo said he tips more than that in the men's room. And that's how he lived.

He did endorse some products. I started working as his accountant and financial advisor shortly after he finished a series of award-winning commercials for Schlitz beer. I later learned that he was so difficult to deal with in making the commercials that Schlitz didn't want to do any more business with him.

Leo could be a real charmer and the world's greatest salesman, but he could also be his own worst enemy. I wouldn't say I helped him change all that, but I did try to have a sobering effect on him, and I do believe I reached him after awhile. At least he'd hear me out on a lot of things.

I got a call one day from a lawyer in New York telling me that the underwear company, Jockey, wanted Leo to appear in some print ads for them. The fee, he said, was $3,500. The ads were going to run in *Sport* magazine and in *Sports Illustrated*, and then they'd see where they would go from there. All Leo had to do was one photo shoot.

I told the attorney this was a complete waste of time, that I knew Leo well enough to know he wasn't going to do commercials for Jockey shorts. I told him thanks for the call, but it wasn't going to happen. It just didn't fit the type of thing Leo would do.

Leo doesn't have to wear the Jockey shorts, the lawyer told me. It wasn't what today would be thought of as a Jim Palmer-type ad. I said he's still not going to do it, but I'll talk to him. So, I call Leo because I felt obligated to pass this proposal along, and he started screaming at me. I remember just holding my phone about three feet away from my ear. He said that's the craziest thing he ever heard. I said I told the lawyer you weren't going to do it. Then he says, well, don't tell him that. Instead of $3,500, he says, tell them I want $5,000. They'll say no, Leo says, and then you'll be done with it.

Now I'm confused. I say, Leo, if you don't want to do it, you don't want to do it. Why go through this? Harvey, just tell them $5,000, Leo assures me. I realize he's trying to make a game of this whole thing. And he did.

I call the attorney back and say Leo doesn't want to do it, but $5,000 would get him to think about it. The man says, we can't do that, never mind, forget it. Three or four days later I get another call from Jockey saying, we'll give you the $5,000.

I call Leo and say now look what you've gotten yourself into. He says, I'm still not going to do it. Tell them I want 10. I say, Leo, I'm not going to play this game. He says tell them 10. I call the man at Jockey back and tell him he ought to forget it, this is an exercise in futility, we're playing a game. Then I tell him Leo said he would do it for 10. Understandably, the man lost his temper a little bit. I said, look, don't yell at me, this is your own doing. Why don't we just forget the whole thing?

To make a long story short, the pattern continued and we finally turned down $15,000. They went that high because their campaign was a series of sports personalities and they desperately needed one more, a baseball manager. Since Leo was the most famous, they were willing to keep going after him.

After we turned down $15,000, however, they had had enough. The man called back and said, it's over, we just got Hank Bauer, manager of the Kansas City Athletics. We don't need Leo. I said that's fine, we'll just forget about it. But we couldn't. Hank Bauer was fired a day or two later, and they lost interest in using him after that.

They called me back and said we want to make a deal. What do you want? I said $25,000. They said okay. What started at $3,500 had become $25,000. Maybe Leo knew what he was doing all along, and maybe he didn't. But we had a deal.

They wanted Leo to come to New York for the photo shoot. I said, he's not coming to New York. He's too busy managing the Cubs. So, they sent a whole crew to Chicago on a Friday after a game. The shoot went into Saturday and was finished later in the day. In the meantime, the lawyer in New York sent me the contract, and it was not at all what it was supposed to be.

For instance, one section of the contract stipulated two commercials a year for two years rather than only one year. For some reason, the lawyer for Jockey had signed the contract already, something the contractor should never do first. I called Leo and said these contracts are wrong. He said, well, I'm all done, they've got the commercials.

I contacted the lawyer and began to explain. He said, that's just too bad. You got 25,000 bucks, he says, that's the least you can do. I said, the $25,000 is not our problem. The contract is totally unacceptable, and we're not going to sign it. He said, I don't care. We've got the commercials.

I said, okay, if you want to play that way, you've got the commercials, but I've got a contract signed by you. If you run those commercials without our signature, you'll get sued for a lot more than $25,000. He said, I've never signed a contract first in my life. I said, you have now. I'm not the type of person who lies about things, so you've got to figure out if I'm bluffing. I said, if you run the commercials, we'll sue you. If you don't run the commercials, when the time is up I'll sign the contract, and then you'll owe us the money. He finally blinked. He said okay, sent us the right contract, which we signed, and they eventually ran the commercials. Leo got his $25,000.

I'm not sure what he did with the money, but I remember Ellen and I went out to dinner with Lynne and Leo soon after and Lynne showed us some jewelry from David Webb in New York. It was a necklace and a pair of earrings. It was something like 20 carats of diamonds and emeralds in the necklace and matching earrings. When Lynne showed them to Ellen, who happens to know a lot about jewelry, Lynne said, the nice thing about the jewelry is they're very practical. What she meant was you could take the earrings and make them into a pin, or you could wear one without the other or something like that. But Ellen looked at Lynne, and said, "Lynne, don't give me practical. You tell me how they turn into a hide-a-bed. That's practical."

It was, first of all, much more than anybody should have spent, and I knew Leo couldn't really afford it, but he was very much in love with Lynne, and he spent money like that all the time. I tried to make sure he didn't carry much money on him, because he'd burn a hole in his pocket.

I represented Leo when he signed his contract with the Cubs in 1966. We put in a provision that in addition to his contract, Mr. Wrigley would give Leo $10,000 as a personal gift for various business expenses for things Leo needed to do as manager of the Cubs. During the disastrous 1969 season I got a call from the Internal Revenue Service wanting to know why Leo hadn't picked that up on his income tax return. I told them it was not taxable, but they said they were advised by the

Cubs that it was. I had a copy of the contract showing that it wasn't taxable and made an appointment to see John Holland, who was the general manager of the Cubs at that time, so he could confirm it with the IRS. I explained it to him and he said basically, look, I don't want to talk about this until the season's over. I told him we don't have time for that, but he said, you tell Leo that's his problem.

Well, that wasn't very smart of Holland because, first of all, he was wrong, and, secondly, that wasn't the way to deal with Leo. I mentioned to Leo that I wasn't going to be able to handle this right now unless we got to Mr. Wrigley. Leo went on a tirade, tore into Holland's office, and told him what he thought. Holland in turn called Wrigley, who acknowledged it was a gift. We solved the problem, but it was amazing to me how something of really no significance got blown way out of proportion and became a continuing irritant between Durocher and Holland.

During that time, I knew a gentleman named Gil Blechman, who was running a paper carton company. He ended up selling his business to Stone Container. Gil had some pretty good success in hiring athletes, either while they were playing or at the end of their careers, and teaching them the business. He was smart enough to realize that an athlete, even a very famous one, could only go so far on his name. But he knew that an athlete's name could open doors, and if he were willing to work hard an athlete could become very successful for himself and the company. Gil told me to let him know if I knew of any Cubs' players who were looking to do something that would lead to a secure future. I mentioned this to Durocher one day at Wrigley Field and, I remember, he stopped practice, called the whole infield in — Banks, Beckert, Kessinger and Santo — sat them down and said, "Harvey's got a helluva deal for you guys. You all ought to do what he says." Nobody ever did, but the fact that Leo made such a big production of what was just a little favor showed his true colors. He wouldn't just look out for his friends, he'd dominate whatever he got involved in. He was an incredibly powerful personality, and that may have been as much a cause of his downfall as it was his success.

I started investing for him, and for a long time he was accumulating a good amount of money and living well. Between his pension, social security and investments, I had him on what I thought was a pretty good line.

I think in that sense alone I did some good things for Leo. Of course, this relationship was working out for me as well.

Everybody seemed to know I represented Leo. I could walk into Wrigley Field whenever I wanted. He'd always leave me some tickets for any game, but I could also go downstairs and sit in the manager's office. That's where I met a lot of famous ball players. I got to know coaches Amalfitano and Herman Franks very well. Franks ended up getting involved with an accountant in Salt Lake City, Utah, who played the real estate game very well. Franks became a very wealthy man and brought a lot of athletes into a number of his deals.

I remember going to spring training in Arizona one year. Leo gave me the uniform of Darcy Fast, number 38. Darcy was a young left-handed pitcher who had either just been released or was injured. I walked around spring training with this uniform on for a couple of days, and people would ask me for my autograph. I didn't know what to do. I just kept telling people, "After the game, after the game...."

To many, Leo was considered one of the greatest manager's the game has ever seen. Of course, he wasn't a bad shortstop either. After beginning with the New York Yankees, where his teammates included Lou Gehrig and Babe Ruth, he moved on to become one of the Gashouse Gang with the St. Louis Cardinals. When Leo moved on to become player/manager of the Brooklyn Dodgers' teams of the 1940s, he really seemed to find his calling. Later, as manager of Brooklyn's arch-rivals, the New York Giants, Leo led the team to the 1951 championship, one of the most exciting victories of all time, fueled by Bobby Thomson's legendary home run. Leo was a fighter and a winner, and today he's remembered more for his managing skills than his impressive playing career.

One year while managing the Cubs, Leo was invited to attend a Major League Baseball dinner announcing the results of their poll to determine the most outstanding manager of all time. Leo was one of three candidates, who included Casey Stengel and Walter Alston.

Almost everyone felt Casey Stengel would win, and he did, but it was certainly an honor to be considered in this group. Leo planned to attend and, because I was still representing Ticketron and they thought it would be wise to take a table at the event, I made plans to go. The theory, from Ticketron's point of view, was that these potential connections with various baseball executives might help Ticketron get its ticket service into all the major league ball parks. I attended the dinner as a representative of Ticketron, not as a representative of Leo.

Leo was sitting at the head table with the other candidates. Former ball player Tony Kubek was the master of ceremonies. I remember Kubek had a handful of index cards guiding his presentation. As he referred to the cards he introduced the candidates, offering background and praise on their incredible careers. But he never mentioned Leo's name, never talked of his career and never introduced him.

I was very confused because I knew Tony had nothing against Leo. This just didn't make any sense. After the dinner was over I was talking to Leo when Kubek came over. Tony said, "Leo, I've got to apologize." He went on to say he felt sick about this, that he didn't realize he hadn't mentioned Leo until after the dinner, when he looked down to find an index card with Leo's name on it lying on the floor. "I completely forgot," he said. "It is an inexcusable thing on my part, and I'm sorry." Leo mumbled something gruffly. You could tell he wasn't too happy.

I have no doubt, frankly, that Tony was telling the truth. There could be no reason not to. After all, they didn't nominate Leo as one of the three outstanding managers of all time and then go out of their way to ignore or embarrass him. Mistakes happen, and that was one of them. But Leo didn't take things like that very well, and he was extremely angry. I assumed he'd get over it.

Lynne had two daughters and a son. In the middle of the Cubs' pennant run, Lynne decided to send her son Joel to Camp Ojibwa, my father-in-law's camp up in Eagle River, Wisconsin. Ellen and my daughters were up there at the same time and I remember it was just after the fiasco at the baseball awards dinner and Leo said he'd really like to get up to visit Joel the next weekend. We talked about it and decided to charter a plane out of Meigs Field in Chicago in the late afternoon, after the Cubs' game, and return Sunday morning before the next game.

We planned to leave at about 4:30 or 5 p.m. I would be in my office, so when the game was finished Leo was going to get a cab and pick Lynne and me up there, then we'd go over to Meigs.

So, it's Saturday and I'm sitting in my office at about 2:30 or 3 in the afternoon, which means the game was in the middle innings. Just then I get a call from Leo, who says, "Harvey, call up Meigs and get the plane, we're leaving now." What are you talking about? I ask him. You can't do that. You're in the middle of a game. Leo says, in effect, I don't care. He says we're going up. "I want to make sure I make dinner." I couldn't talk him out of it, and he said he wasn't feeling well anyway, so he was going.

This whole thing was supposed to be a secret in the first place, although Mr. Wrigley probably wouldn't have had a problem if Leo had stuck to the original plan. This, however, was a bold move that was sure to mean trouble. We got up to Eagle River at about 4:30 p.m., had dinner and stayed overnight. Lynne, Leo and I flew back at about 9:30 Sunday morning, in plenty of time for the Cubs' afternoon game. But as we were about to land, Leo looked at me and said, "I'm not going to the game." He told me to call Joey Amalfitano when we landed, and to tell him Leo wouldn't be there, or to call the ball park and tell them Leo was sick and that Joey should manage the game.

I couldn't believe it. I looked at him and said, "Why are you doing this? You're not sick. So what's the matter with you?" Leo said, well, major league baseball didn't need me last week. I don't need them this weekend. Apparently he was more hurt by the events of the awards dinner than even I thought. He still perceived it as intended snub. As wrong as I think he was, he was sure he was right, and this is how he planned to get even.

Everything seemed to be kept under wraps until a newspaper in Wisconsin published a photo of a sign that hung on the wall of one of the companies in Eagle River. It read,

"Welcome to Eagle River, Leo Durocher."

Of course, it all came out that Leo was up there seeing Lynne's son, that he had left in the middle of a game and that he didn't make the game on Sunday. That was, I think, the beginning of the end of his relationship with Mr. Wrigley. It was sad because I think the night in Eagle River was a very special evening for Leo. He saw a lot of boys, spoke at the dinner and seemed to have a great time. Had he followed the schedule, no one would have cared. But Leo had to get even.

It's no secret that, over the years, Frank Sinatra became one of Leo's closest friends. Leo ended his career in 1973 as manager of the Houston Astros. He moved to Palm Springs, and he and Frank saw quite a bit of each other.

From what I know, it was kind of an on-and-off relationship. Maybe that's how Sinatra was with everybody, but when Leo became sick at one point, Frank took him into his home and took care of him. This was after Leo had gotten divorced from Lynne and didn't really have anyone else.

I remember a time when they weren't getting along very well, and Leo said it was just making him sick that Frank wouldn't talk to him, that he wouldn't let Leo get anywhere near him. Anywhere he goes, Leo would say, I can't be there. He'd go on and on about it.

Some years before, I met Frank Sinatra when Triangle Productions brought him in to do concerts in Chicago, Cleveland and Detroit, but I doubted that he remembered me. I once went on an "advance mission" to scout out Cobo Hall in Detroit, where Frank was going to perform. Frank's bodyguard accompanied me to check out the place as well. When we were through I told him we'd better get going because we had a plane to catch. He wouldn't budge. He said not to worry, they would hold the plane for us. We finally got to the airport at departure time. Frank's bodyguard told the attendant who he was and who he worked for. We watched the plane take off without us. I guess that's just the way people think when they're convinced they are very important — that they can control everything.

Finally, with Leo continuing to go on about Frank, I decided to call Mickey Rudin. Rudin was, for many years, Frank Sinatra's lawyer. I told Mickey I didn't know if there was anything he could do, but I wanted him to know Leo was really despondent about the deterioration of his relationship with Frank. I was sure Leo wasn't going to do anything traumatic, but I just thought if Rudin got the chance to mention it to Frank, maybe we could encourage them to patch things up.

Mickey said, look, I've known Leo a long time now, and I'm sure he's not going to kill himself over this. Then he told me about an aunt of his who ruined his parents' lives. He said she threatened to commit suicide almost every day. He said he remembered sitting at the dinner table as a kid and "we'd get a call, and my mother would leave and run over to my aunt's apartment to check on her." This went on for years and years. He said one Christmas he went home to New York for the holidays. "We're all sitting around, and my aunt says to me, 'Mickey, I feel terrible.'" Mickey asked, about what? She said, well, I intended to knit you a sweater for Christmas, but I just haven't been able to get it done. I feel awful. Mickey said, well, don't worry about it. It's warm out in California. I've got plenty of sweaters. And she said, no, you don't understand, Mickey. She said as soon as she finished that sweater she was going to kill herself. Mickey said, well, don't hurry because I don't really need the sweater. About two months later he got a box in the mail with his Christmas sweater, and the next day his aunt killed herself. After all that he told me he hoped Leo wasn't at that point. He wasn't, and his friendship with Frank was soon repaired.

There was a night back when Leo was still in baseball — he was managing Houston at the time — when I got a call at about 3 a.m. He woke me out of a deep sleep and I eventually realized it was Leo. He told me to jump on a plane and get out there. He was in Las Vegas and he said he had just won $25,000 gambling. "I want you to get out here with a suitcase, put the money in it and then put it in a safety deposit box."

I was awake by now and told him I'm not doing that. That's when I asked who he was with, and he said, Sinatra. I said that's great, how many people saw you win that money? He said I don't know, all kinds of people. I said I'll tell you what you do, give the money over to the hotel and they'll give you a check or a credit for it. Hold onto that money because you need it, we're going to put it on your tax return, and that's just the way it's going to be. With that he started screaming at me, saying nobody does that, and I'm not about to pay taxes on this. I said, yes, you are. First of all, you are because you have to. Secondly, you are because of who you are. Third, you are because of who you're with. He ended up doing exactly that.

Years later Bowie Kuhn, who was commissioner of baseball at that time and who for some reason never much liked Leo, called Leo and Lynne in one day for a meeting. It had some kind of reminiscent overtones of the old Happy Chandler days when Leo was suspended from baseball for ostensibly associating with gamblers. I talked to Leo about that episode a couple of times, and even at the end of his life he was bitter about it. He believed, as do many others, that he was either framed, set up or used as an example. Either way, he viewed it as a tragic time of his life.

In any case, Bowie Kuhn tried to pin something on him along the same lines, referring to his Las Vegas trip, and saying he was sure that Leo had not reported his winnings on his income tax return. Leo, of course, showed him that he had.

Leo wrote a book some years later in which he recounted the story. In typical Leo fashion, he said, not only did I pay income tax on that money, but from the beginning I insisted to my accountant, Harvey Wineberg, that he pick it up as income on my tax return.

Apparently that was one of the incidents that led to a further breakdown in the Durocher-Sinatra relationship. Frank thought he was either loaning Leo some money or that Leo had taken some money from him without Sinatra knowing it. It's hard for me to believe that, but somehow Frank thought that Leo had done something wrong, and so for another year they didn't talk to each other. But they eventually worked things out again.

Because I tried to keep personal contact with Leo, I remember Ellen and I went out to see him in California one week. This just happened to be when Sinatra was celebrating his birthday, which meant we were invited to his home along with a number of famous people.

The first night we went out to dinner and then back to Sinatra's house. The second night he cooked dinner at his house, and the third night — it was a long celebration — there was a party for him up in the hills. Sinatra rented a bus, and we all went up there to somebody's house. Jimmy Van Heusen played the piano and Sinatra sang a lot of old-time favorites, which kind of reminded me in many ways of the days I spent listening to the old-time folk songs. It was, obviously, an exciting evening.

I was working awfully hard in those days and planned to

leave the next day. I remember Sinatra saying there was one more dinner the next night and that we had to be there. I said, "I can't, Frank. I've got to get back. I've got a million problems, and travel plans have already been made." He said, one more day, Harvey, and again I said, I'm sorry, but I can't. He looked at me and said, have you ever been visited by anybody who when they left your nose was kind of mashed in and your ears were kind of bent back and you had cement on your shoes? Ever have that happen? I said, don't start with me, I've got to leave. He laughed, and I left, and that's the last time I saw him.

I do have a picture of Sinatra down in my basement, though. Actually, my basement is filled with pictures of people I've been involved with over the years. It's quite a collection. When we took the picture of Ellen and me with Sinatra, right before they snapped it Frank said, all right, nobody smiles. Of course, whatever he said you did, so there's this picture of the three of us looking like we've just come from a funeral.

Speaking of funerals, Leo seemed to be wary of his. There was a time when he insisted his birth certificate made him older than he really was.

As you may know, you can draw your social security at either age 62 or 65. If you draw it at 62, you commit to a lesser figure over the remaining years of your life. Leo was still working at 62, but at 65 he wasn't. If you are 65 and working, you can't draw social security until you're 70, so Leo was eligible for it.

I said to him, "Leo, we're going to apply for social security, and you can start getting it as soon as you turn 65, which is in a couple of months." Harvey, he said, I'm only going to be 64. No, you're not, you're going to be 65. I've got your birth certificate right here. He said he didn't care. "I've told everybody that I'm 64, and I am 64," he said. "That birth certificate's probably wrong." Everything that you've ever done shows you were born when it says here, I said, and you're going to get $18,000 or something a year in social security. Why would you turn that down? "Because I'm not 65," he snapped, "and I'm not taking it." So, we went a whole year without getting social security that we were entitled to.

Leo's later years were fairly lonely ones. He had gotten divorced from Lynne some years before. I served as third party to their meeting at the Beverly Wilshire in Los Angeles, when the two of them had it out about how the divorce would come down. It was one of the least pleasant days of my life.

Leo lived in his Palm Springs apartment and didn't seem to have many friends. He did, however, have a lot of pictures of famous people on the walls — Sinatra, Babe Ruth, the Gashouse Gang among them. We would visit him once in awhile. He didn't do much, just went for walks. One of my visits came a few weeks before he died.

I have a condo on the Gulf in Long Boat Key, Florida, where I try to break up the winter. I was there when I got a call from a doctor at Desert Hospital in Palm Springs saying that I was the designated decision-maker on Leo's Living Will. When I saw Leo just a few weeks before he was in pretty good shape, so I had no reason to expect this call. Apparently he had taken a turn for the worse, his brain stem had broken and the doctor said he needed my permission to, in effect, pull the plug.

I asked if there was any hope at all. He said no, it's impossible, we just need you to tell us it's okay. I said, okay, but then he said there was a problem. Leo is connected to some lifesaving equipment, he explained, and I can't do anything without going to the head of the ethics department at the hospital, but I need your permission first.

The whole thing seemed confusing, but it didn't really matter in this case. I got a call a short time later saying Leo had died.

I guess the moral of the story is that these decisions should be made before you're hooked up. They don't have any problem not hooking you up, but they have a problem unhooking you. Why I didn't get the call at that time, before they hooked him up, is still a mystery to me.

Leo was a very important person in my life. His obituary explained he was important to others as well. Although recognized as somewhat of a complicated person, he was remembered as a good one. To my knowledge, he always sought to be good to people, and to be good for people. He never lost, he just got beat. That's what made him a winner.

Leo's former wife, Lorraine Day, and he had long ago adopted a son and a daughter who Leo stayed in touch with. Lorraine and her husband arranged for Leo's funeral in Los Angeles. They were very friendly and gracious, nice people.

The funeral itself was all that you would expect, a lot of famous people from baseball and some celebrities from Hollywood. I was there to mourn, but I was also the executor of Leo's estate. I hired an attorney in Palm Springs to handle the legal affairs out there, and I took care of finishing off his estate. Leo's two children, of course, were the beneficiaries.

As you can guess, Leo wasn't shy about holding grudges. Later in life he remained bitter about the way he was treated by certain members of the baseball hierarchy. He was upset that he wasn't elected into baseball's Hall of Fame, considering his impressive record as both a player and manager. On more than one occasion, he told me if he ever got into the Hall of Fame posthumously that I should turn it down for him. I told him he'd never know. He was eventually elected in. I did not turn it down for him, and he never knew. Obviously, I didn't carry out his wishes because he so deserved the recognition.

Leo left me a small painting to remember him by. He also left me a set of Frank Sinatra's golf clubs that Frank had once given to him. Not only does the bag have Frank's name on it, but all the irons have his name engraved into them. They're still in my garage and someday, when the right moment presents itself, I'll offer them to the right charity with hopes they raise some significant money from them. I think Leo would like that.

CHAPTER VIII
Investing In A Profession

Accounting is like other professions in that if you commit to hard work, dedication, honesty and caring, the rewards justify the efforts. It is also a profession that offers opportunity for a fruitful career for those with the skill and ability it demands.

I think the positives of becoming an accountant are self-evident. There is a significant amount of prestige in such a career, and security for the accountant and his or her family. For me, after 40 years in the business, the overriding reason for being an accountant was the opportunity to maintain my independence. I didn't really want to work for anyone else. Even when I wasn't a partner in or head of a firm, I always felt I was working in a very interesting environment and never working on just one project.

You won't get rich overnight in accounting, but the profession does offer investment opportunities — of course, it always depends on the makeup of the person.

For those majoring in accounting at school, in order to become a CPA there are still the obstacles of taking two-day exams in law, accounting theory, auditing, taxes and so on. Once you get your certificate, you are required to have 40 hours a year of continuing professional education.

At one point, I thought about opening an office in Florida, because I have a number of good friends and clients there. Although that's no longer in the plans, I did pass the Florida exam. That state requires that CPAs take the same amount of hours, but with a greater emphasis on auditing and accounting.

As I've alluded to already, our firm is not interested in or capable of offering the entire spectrum of services. We've chosen to concentrate on small, family owned businesses, professional practices, financial planning, real estate ventures, trusts, estates, profit sharing and income tax work. Many people refer to us as a boutique firm because of our specialized, one-to-one care. I believe that's a reasonably accurate description.

We try to provide people help on investments and investment planning, although we never promote any investment for our own benefit. We feel strongly that if we know about an investment opportunity that fits the needs of our clients, we try to fit the two sides together.

We like to say, what you don't plan for in December, will come back to haunt you in April. We also believe it's just as easy to stay caught up as it is to stay two or three months behind. I think those are two of our overriding feelings that we try to convey to our clients. We also back it up with current, relevant information and financial planning that includes long-term security information and investment planning.

There is obviously no substitute for building relationships with your clients that allow you to understand their lives or their businesses. That is what we mean by being proactive, and if every day we make one positive contribution to better someone's financial security or their net worth, then I feel it's been a very worthwhile day.

I recently received a report from my internist doctor that illustrates the way we approach our services. Dr. Ron Semerdjian, who has been a client of mine for years and was President of Professional Standards and chief of the Pulmonary Section at Evanston Hospital, provided me with a very impressive output. It was basically an annual report of my physical condition — fortunately a very positive one — and it outlined to both doctor and patient the status of my health. What we do for people is offer them a financial physical examination. If we don't cover everything that's happened within the year and show how the client's overall financial health can and should improve, then I don't feel we've done a very thorough examination.

Recently, there's been a lot of discussion about the untenable complexity of the Internal Revenue Code. Are they right? You bet. Is it a mess? It sure is. I've spent many restless and sleepless nights worrying about tax matters of all kinds, and even though I have reference materials at home, it's not until I get to the office and research it fully and talk it out with my partners that I can sometimes get comfortable with our position(s). It can be a nightmare. But, are there better alternatives? I don't think so — and not just for selfish reasons.

Representative Dick Armey's (R-Texas) and Steve Forbes'

flat tax proposal just doesn't seem to make much sense. Their typical approach would eliminate some or all deductions, including the one for cherished mortgage interest, and apply a lower rate, say 17%, instead of 28% for the average person. Why is that simpler? You still have to compute income, which is always the major problem. And we know how to multiply by different numbers.

The same goes for Representative Bill Archer (R-Texas) and Representative Bill Tanzins' (R-Louisiana) proposal for a "no tax" system, replacing the income tax system with either a 15% national sales tax or a national value-added tax (VAT) at 17.5%. The VAT requires policing and auditing at almost every step of the manufacturing process, clearly not a simple task and clearly not easy to implement, for many reasons.

In both cases, it's the lower and middle class income tax payers who get hurt the worst. They're already hurt badly by regressive payroll taxes — young people in their own businesses get killed by the self-employment tax. You don't have to look back any further than the 1996 presidential election, when the populace obviously saw the Forbes proposal as a help-the-rich scheme. I heard just recently that Forbes' taxes would have been cut by more than half under his plan. I just can't imagine this kind of proposal being accepted here in our lifetime. In addition, the logistical difficulties of moving from one tax system to another in an economy of the size and complexity of the United States could prove insurmountable.

An alternative, of course, would be a gross income tax, which, I believe, they tried in Indiana where it didn't work. It would be taxing someone who sold a building for a million dollars on that amount, even though the building may have cost him or her a million dollars. He or she would have to pay tax on the gross receipts. The inequities there appear to be obvious, so I can't see any good alternatives to an income tax, as imperfect as it may be.

If you want a real nightmare, try the states' income tax laws. Most states (and a few cities) have tax laws that are all different. Florida and Texas, amongst the big states, have no income tax, but Florida has an intangible tax on securities, which is tough but not too onerous.

If you work in a state on a "physical presence" basis, or if you sell property situated in that state, they want a return and taxes from you. To make the extreme point, a professional athlete may play in 10 taxing states and have to file with each state on the income earned in them. He or she then gets a proportionate credit on his or her "home state" return for taxes paid to the other states — New York and California are the worst. Not only are their "residency tests" extremely difficult, but their rates are the highest, which means you lose a lot of those taxes as a credit. The rest, of course, are deductible against federal taxes. Fun, right? Thank goodness for the computer.

It's not too dissimilar from the federal situation with foreign countries. If you're a U.S. citizen or have a green card, you must pick up your world income on your U.S. return and then take credit for foreign taxes paid. We once had an athlete playing in Italy (not Vinnie) and his team said not to worry, they'd take care of his taxes. Not a good idea — they were going to reduce his income by the taxes they paid for him (it didn't matter to them), but we would have had to pick up the net income with no tax form and, therefore, no credit for taxes. They finally did it right.

People are obviously becoming more long-term security conscious. There are different kinds of retirement planning opportunities: IRAs (which changed dramatically under the

1997 Revenue Act, with many new opportunities, including the Roth and Educational IRAs), Keoghs, 401(k)s, pensions and regular and defined benefit profit-sharing plans. It's how people are going to be able to provide for their overall security. Now that we're all living longer, it's even more crucial.

It used to be that people would work up to age 65 and then live 10 more years or so. Now people are living into their 80s and 90s with greater frequency, and that means they have to be provided for. The government, I think, is recognizing that by not forcing you to take your retirement funds until you are at least 70 and a half years old. Whatever you do, don't take your retirement funds before you have to. A rule of thumb used to be if the youngest of the spouses had an eight-year actuarial life and you were averaging 8% or more on your money, unless both parties were ill, you'd be statistically better off waiting. With the recent repeal of the 15% excise tax, that's even truer. If it's done right, elder people ought to be financially stable and able to live and die with dignity.

Since I began my career as a certified public accountant, taxes and investments have changed dramatically. Just before I started, the highest tax rates were 90%. Contrast that with the early part of the century — I have an old tax return in my office that shows that in 1914, the first time there was an income tax, the lowest rate was 1%, going to 6% on $500,000 of income.

All things are relative, of course. Just as it would be difficult to compare Babe Ruth's salary to those of modern day baseball players, it would be silly to rely too much on comparisons to our early tax structure. There is no question, however, that the 1% to 6% rates from back then are not equivalent to today's high rates.

Shortly after I started in taxes, the top rate was 70%, then it went down to 50%. Since then, it has gone to 28% and back up to where it is now. The top rate is 39.6%, but the equivalent rate when you adjust for all kinds of disallowances is over 40%. As the written tax laws have changed, of course, so have people's investment philosophies.

Sheltered in the 1970s and 1980s

Back in the 1970s and early 1980s, tax shelters were in their heyday. I have a wooden trinket on my desk that one of my daughters' friends gave me. It has a little wooden roof over some thumb tacks and says, "That's the last of the tax shelters." Wineberg and Lewis never went into the tax shelter business, but a man named Sam Zell did.

You probably have heard of Zell and his Equity Properties. His company is one of the most powerful real estate ventures in the world. In those early days, Sam was promoting, let's say, two-for-one tax shelters on what was hopefully a good investment. He, for the most part, dealt in residential, but also did some commercial real estate. I don't believe he ever got involved in industrial real estate. But he and his partner, Bob Lurie, were like a tag team. They were really close and Bob was the financial expediter, you might say. At the time, he put a number of people, including myself, into some of Sam's apartment properties.

Although our checks were not late, one day Bob walked over to pick them up. I had no idea what he looked like at the time, so when I saw this kind of scraggly man with a long beard I thought he was a messenger. Those were the days when the corporate culture wore jeans.

In any case, a two-for-one shelter, such as his, meant that you could put the same money into the deal that you would have given to the government. We did that from the late

1970s to 1986, when the tax laws changed.

The laws changed because some people were abusing the system, which always happens, causing the most protective measures to be taken. I was told by two "in" people that the Senate Finance Committee tried to make a deal with the real estate developers, particularly in New York, to be more reasonable in their attitudes. But the really big hitters wouldn't give in at all, so they put it to them — so to speak — in a big way.

Facing New Changes

In 1986, a law was passed which, in effect, eliminated all of the shelters. You had to be at risk, and you also had to have passive income in order to use the real estate passive losses created. There was a phase out for a few years that helped, but because you could no longer deduct those losses against your ordinary income, this change was greatly responsible for the real estate recession of the late 1980s and early 1990s. There were, of course, a lot of deeper shelters besides real estate — five to one, seven to one, nine to one, and a lot of credits. The government always questions whether to pump the economy to get certain industries moving. There were energy credits, double energy credits and all kinds of investment credits. Some of those credits were renewed, but the people who invested in movies, books and windmills, had huge write-offs in the early years and huge recaptures once the bottoms fell out of those markets, which they did.

At the time, we were into real estate, which was what I was weaned on because in my old firm that's pretty much what we did, and what I knew best. But we knew there had to be alternatives, and in those days people were very interested in precious metals. Gold was $34 an ounce before they lifted the restrictions and it shot up to over $800. We had some people who bought it in the middle hundreds and got some good rises out of it. Many people were buying gold on the theory that you had a hedge against disaster. I had a client who asked me to buy gold for him on one of my trips to Europe to see the First National Bank in Switzerland, which I did.

The officer at that bank — a real "dooms-sayer" — was sending letters to people encouraging them to convert all of their assets to either gold or silver and to pick up their families and move to either Western Canada or Australia, wherever you could be self-sufficient and work the land. I read later that he lost his job, which wasn't surprising.

Once the new tax reform act was passed, one of the other industries that remained tax benefited was the gas and oil industry. Larry Fleisher, an impressive man who was the head of the National Basketball Players Association and with whom I had somewhat of a relationship, introduced us to two gentlemen from New York who were representing some gas explorers and developers on the Gulf Coast off of Houston. We spent 1986 to 1990 involved in gas exploration deals with them. It started out quite well, but didn't end up that well. A lot of people were unhappy, but we had a strong cohesive group and when things started to go wrong, we hired an attorney and threatened to sue the promoters. Without going into all of the details, we thought they had misrepresented themselves to us, as well as to many other people, including major companies, foundations and educational institutions. Although some venturers lost money, our group came out getting almost everything back. With additional tax benefits by virtue of sustained depletion and excess intangible drilling costs, we may have come out even, or a little bit ahead. That certainly wasn't the intent, but at the time it seemed like one of the better alternatives.

Our clients have had excellent results with David Hovey's Optima, Inc., a North Shore developer. He is just finishing a 400-unit manor home, townhouse and condominium development (almost a little city) in Deerfield, Illinois, called Coromandel. The name comes from a famous scenic peninsula in his native New Zealand.

Deciding On Stocks

These changes left, of course, the security market — either debt or equity. I was never really strong on investing in the stock market, probably for two reasons. When I was growing up, I never had any real money and wasn't exposed to it the way others might have been. I didn't know a lot about it and was concerned that people would rely on me beyond my knowledge. The other reason is best explained by the comments of Professor Jeremy Siegel, who spoke at a seminar we recently co-sponsored.

Seigel was, at that time, a professor at Wharton College and had been at both the University of Chicago and Harvard. He brought out charts and charts, claiming he was the only one who had charted the stock market back to the early 1800s. He came to the conclusion that there is no other market that has out performed inflation as effectively as the equity market. He claims the only time that that wasn't the case was in a fifteen year period from 1966 to 1981. What he meant was not that the market didn't do as well as inflation, but that in relation to inflation, fixed instruments did better.

But that's a pretty long time to ponder, particularly when you're not sure when it's going to end. Obviously, that was the main time of my practice, and I remember in those days clients were switching investment advisors all over the place.

It was a game of musical chairs.

I went up to the Professor after the presentation and asked, "If this was 1976 instead of 1996, would you still be saying the same thing?" He said, "I would have, given all the research that I now have in front of me. The difference is that, in 1976, no one would have been here to listen."

Today, however, it seems there really is no better alternative than being as heavy in the equity market as one can be. No real tax strategies are left to be played. Anybody who is taking full advantage of retirement plans and, where applicable, defined benefit plans that allow people to put away the greatest possible dollars based on their life expectancies, is probably doing as much as they can to beat the tax man. The right investment approach now is to convert an ordinary income rate of over 40%, to a capital gain rate of 20%, which eventually goes to 18%. Our theory is that if people are widely diversified between small cap and large cap and growth and value, and have X% in international funds and emerging markets, none of which is overly profound, but all of which is very sensible, then that's the best they can do. This approach can also be augmented by hedge fund investing where applicable.

We don't pick stocks, but when clients request assistance we do try to put people with proper investment advisors. Under any normal circumstances, people ought to average 10% after fees. If you can do that at capital gain rates, don't try to time the market and let the growth appreciate tax free, well, that's the plan. Try to invest in high quality stocks with relatively low dividends, and stay out of dividend-paying funds so the bulk of your returns would be in appreciation.

One of the most significant changes in estate planning involves the interplay between life insurance and various kinds of charitable lead trusts. For years I have been the accountant for a major charitable foundation that has multi-million dollars in it. One of the requirements for reporting on private foundations is that you have to not only list the cost of the securities, but the market values. I'm constantly amazed to see that stocks bought in the 1970s and 1980s have just grown and grown. Not to say that the boom in the last few years that took the Dow Jones from 3,000 to 8,000 is going to continue without peril, but I think price-to-earnings ratios are about 18 times and, although there can always be a significant correction, in the long run there is no better alternative to high grade equity investing.

There are two good reasons for most people not to be entirely in equities. The first is, if you ever have to take the money out at the wrong time. And the second, if you just can't sleep at night.

I understand the logic behind this. My feeling is that most people would not feel comfortable being entirely in the market. But long-term, it really is the approach that says, there is no better one for today.

Personal Practice Makes Perfect for Clients

We don't get involved in certified audits. Much of our practice today is being devoted to personal service — which everyone claims to give, but we really do.

That's not to say anything against that fine group of accountants who perform certified audits, but it's not the way we choose to practice. While earnings in most accounting firms are based on a lot of staff work, our practice is built on personal relationships with a lot of people. No single client constitutes more than 2% of our entire practice, which is comforting, but it also means we must and do pay more attention to detail.

Many of these clients faced or are facing the same experiences and obstacles that I have — like maybe getting your children through summer camp, college and weddings, or providing for longer retirement than in years past. Today, anyone who plans on living less than 90 years is probably making a strategic planning mistake.

Maybe that's just my thinking, but I've got a mother who's 92, and a father-in-law who is 96. I can tell you it's very comforting for me to know that they're financially very sound — they don't need my help; people don't want to need anyone's help.

Much of our practice is dedicated to dealing with those types of life issues. We don't have large administrative costs, we don't have layers of review. We have good people who know what they are doing and are subject only to a partner's review. I've said it's just as easy to stay caught up as it is to stay two or three months behind, which is unfortunately the way many people live. Years ago when I was breaking into the business, working ungodly hours and rarely at home, I said to myself, "I hope someday I can have a firm where that doesn't have to be a way of life."

To say that accountants don't have busy tax seasons is as foolish as saying retailers can take off in the month of December. There are often more jobs than there are good accountants, and we're always fighting that battle. It may be because working women who have children don't want to work weekends or nights for three months, or because the investment banking and money management and financial institutions, and the large firms — as well as private industry — are hiring a lot more good people. We've either been smart or lucky in that regard, but I do know that one of our philosophies is we'll get through the season successfully, without killing ourselves. That way I believe we'll do better work and, without trying to be overly paternalistic, help take care of our people.

Profit sharing, medical reimbursements and any other tax advantage benefits that are allowed should be utilized. Having four daughters ranging between the ages of 28 and 34, I understand how hard it is for younger people to save very much — payroll taxes being almost as onerous as income taxes. I also know that same age group would love to get every dollar they can right now and "worry about tomorrow tomorrow," but I do think they should start saving as soon as they can, even if they have to start adjusting their present life a little bit. Hopefully, someday, they'll be grateful that was part of the plan.

Although I'm grateful that my plan to become an accountant has paid off both emotionally and financially, I must admit I always possessed a special interest in the law. In fact, I long held a secret wish to be a lawyer.

Even though I knew deep down that I would never practice law, as such, I always felt that I'd pursue a law degree if the right opportunity came along. I'm the type of person who needs answers that are definitive. I get no bigger thrill than making something balance, and that isn't the way it works in law. Still, I was drawn to learn more about it.

I was 43 at the time. It was a Saturday and for some reason I was walking by the Northwestern Law School on the near north side of Chicago. I passed the law school building, walked in and just asked someone at the desk when the next LSATs would be given. The woman told me they were going to be given soon, and she handed me an application.

I figured I had nothing to lose by filling it out. A short time later I took the LSAT exam and, although I hadn't taken an exam in 20-some years, I did very well, so well that I figured I might actually have a chance of getting into law school.

At that time I had a lot of limitations on where I could go. I had a full-time job that I was working too hard at. I had a full-time family with four young daughters, and my friend, Shelley Fink, asked if I could take over doing a lot of the tax returns at the Sonnenschein law firm. They had been using a big firm and were unhappy with personnel changes. They weren't really getting the personal attention, and I agreed to do it.

Their offices were in the Sears Tower on the south end of the Loop, and my office is on the north side of the Loop. Kent Law School, which is a division of Illinois Institute of Technology, sat between my office and their offices at Sears Tower, so I applied there, and got accepted.

Before I did anything else, however, I sat down with the dean of the law school and told him my situation, wondering if he would think I was crazy or not. I know I did not want to go at night because I figured I wouldn't go. If I did go, I'd have guilt forever because I was working so hard that I didn't see the kids as much as I would like to and this would certainly prevent me from getting home while they were awake. I told the dean all of that.

I may not have made as many family dinners as I would've liked, but I tried to make almost all of my kids' extra activities — from teacher's meetings to field day to pom pon events. I really felt that was as much my responsibility as anything else, but I also truly enjoyed being there.

They had a rule at that time that you could be a day school student if you took at least 10 hours. So, that's what I did, I signed up for the day school on the dean's advice. It's kind of an interesting thing you're doing, he said. One of three things will happen. Either you'll get sick of this and drop out, or you'll do poorly and we'll throw you out, or somehow you'll find a way to get through, which I did. My theory on this whole approach was that, since they didn't take attendance in most law school classes, it probably wasn't that important to go to class. What was important, I thought, was to read everything. I didn't even bother to check that fallacious thinking with anybody. I just started on that premise, and I remember every morning on the train and every night home on the train and every night when I was home and every weekend all I did was read. I think I ended up going to about a third of the classes.

That was not the right approach because all the time I was in class I was sitting there figuring out where they were, and which case they were on. While I was reading the case ahead I wasn't paying attention to the case being discussed, and the bottom line is what goes on in class is what's important. It's nice to read, but it's much more important to be able to follow class discussions. In any case, I got through. I didn't burn up the league, but I did everything I was supposed to do.

My first year I was in a torts class and at the end of class the professor came up to me and said, "What are you doing here? Are you monitoring this course?" I said, no, I'm a student. I was by far the oldest student.

I tried to take courses that I had some background in that wouldn't be too hard for me to handle, but you obviously don't get through law school taking courses that you're familiar with.

I remember one thing about my law school courses quite vividly. They wouldn't let me take the elementary tax course because I had the CPA background, but they let me take an advanced tax course, which I checked into the very first day and never went to again the whole semester. I showed up for the final exam, which was from 6 to 9 one night. I got there about three minutes to 6, as was my routine, and realized everybody in the room had a tax guide with them. Well, I don't care how much you know about taxes, if you don't have the guide when everybody else does, you're going to have a problem. So, I asked what's going on and someone said, well, it's an open book exam.

Great. The bookstore closed at 6, so I raced down there, bought a guide and raced back up and then started taking the exam. At 9 or so I was finished, but no one else seemed to be leaving or anything, so I reviewed my answers. At 9:15 a couple people left, but when I walked up there and handed the test in, the instructor said that'll be so-many points off your grade. What are you talking about? I said. He explained, well, I said at the beginning that anybody who needs more time can stay later, but for every minute after 9 you're going to lose some points. This sounded kind of crazy to me. I said, look, I didn't hear that. I wasn't here. I had to go buy a book, and I didn't hear that, that's not fair. I've been done since 9, I complained. I've just been sitting there looking things over.

The professor looked at me and said, by the way, who are you? You're not even in this class. I said, yes, I am. He said, I've never seen you. I said I know, so he looked it up and, sure enough, I was registered. I don't know if he ever took the points off because when the grades came out they listed it, and I had the highest mark in the class. That was no big deal, I should have. I was the only one there who had the kind of background I did. After four summers and three years, I finished and looked on to May graduation.

We all went to the graduation, Ellen, the kids, my folks and my in-laws. I was up there on stage and I think I tripped on the step going up, but it was a big thrill for me. My partner, Steve, said it best. He said that "was quite an accomplishment." I don't know if he remembers saying that, but I do, and I still appreciate it.

In any case, I tried to study for the bar exam, but, as I said, I was working hard. I went to the bar review as best I could, but I wasn't really very well-grounded in everything, having hardly ever gone to class. I took the exam in July, and got the results in October. I did not pass the first time, and it was undoubtedly one of the low days of my life.

I remember just walking around in a daze. There's a procedure they have where if you want to discuss the exam, you can. So, I called this designated attorney and went to meet him the following week. He was a lawyer in a big law firm. He looked at me and he said, I don't know how to tell you this, but you missed passing by one point, on one part, which is all that did you in.

I was angry at the world then, and at them in particular. How could I miss by one point? He showed me the exam, and one 10-point essay question in particular where they gave me a four. I looked at it and said, you mean to say if this four was a five, I would have passed? I know it sounds unbelievable, but he said yes, and I kind of lost it. I said I just think that's unconscionable for somebody who spent the time I did, and the money, to come up short on something so arbitrary, there's something wrong with that. The CPA exam is different. With that exam you don't spend three extra years or thousands of dollars more.

What you really should do next time you take it, he said, is make sure you get enough exercise. That wasn't the right thing to say to me, and I told him so. He said stop worrying about it, you'll pass next time, and I did.

It seems to me there should be a way of accrediting the law schools better than they do. It seems that if you've gotten through a good law school you should be equipped to pass. I'm not one of them, but some people just don't take exams well. That doesn't mean they're not going to be a good lawyer. In any case, once I did pass it, it was like I stopped beating my head against a wall for four years, and I could get on with the rest of my life.

At about the same time, I was becoming heavily involved with the American Civil Liberties Union (ACLU). I later became president of the organization's Illinois division for three years and headed a number of committees. This organization, in my opinion, deserves a special place in American culture. I'm proud to be associated with it, and thankful that my old friends, Burt and Babs Joseph, recommended me for a place on the board.

In my way of thinking, the ACLU is the organization that makes it possible for all other organizations of its kind to exist because, whether you agree with everything the ACLU does or not, they are the conscience of the nation. Everyone says it's an extremely liberal organization. Well, I don't know when it became liberal rather than conservative to defend the Constitution and the Bill of Rights.

I had joined the organization shortly before the Nazis planned their controversial march in Skokie. It was kind of an interesting conundrum for me because my parents lived in Skokie. I was a supporter of the Nazis' right to march, even though all of us felt there was no place in the world for them. But, if they were to be denied their rights, obviously we would all be denied some rights somewhere down the road.

As it happens, all of the courts supported us, from the local courts all the way up to the U.S. Supreme Court. Although we lost a lot of ACLU members during those years, I have no doubt it was one of our finer moments. Ironically, we gained a lot of members when Ed Meese became attorney general, although we'd rather have done it without him.

The pressure we were under was great. Ed Rothschild, who was president at that time and one of the top lawyers in Chicago, was pretty much a moderate, non-hard-line type person, but saw clearly that there was an issue here that was overriding. Ed died a couple years ago. He was one of the really great men I've had the pleasure of knowing. We were lucky to have him at the helm when all of that went down. The current and long-time executive director is Jay Miller, a man I have known for many years. He and Harvey Grossman, the ACLU's chief legal counsel, and his best little law firm in Chicago, are doing a fabulous job of protecting our liberties. With the emergence of dangerous conservative religious rights groups that threaten to upset the separation of church and state, it's most important that we all recognize where the real threats to our liberties lie.

CHAPTER IX
From Camp to Politics

I quickly came to learn that Camp Ojibwa in Eagle River, Wisconsin, is a place like no other. Because it had been run by her father and mother, the camp had long been special to Ellen. But it also became special to the rest of our family, and to the many friends we came to know through our visits.

When the girls were young, they would spend the summers there with Ellen. I would work during the week and then drive up on Fridays and back on Sunday afternoon, Sunday evening or Monday morning. Unfortunately, in those days it was about a five-and-a-half to six-hour ride. But I did it almost every week for the term of the camp, which was eight weeks. At the end of the camp they had what they called a post-camp, where the adults would come up with their families and stay for a week. They were some of the most enjoyable and pleasant summers of our family's life.

I met a lot of people up at the camp who became very important to me. In particular, there were two people who strongly impacted my life. My business partner, Steve Lewis, was one of them. Steve is 15 years younger than me. I was probably 34 when we met. He had gone there as a camper and a junior counselor, and eventually became the camp's tennis counselor.

Because I was up there almost every weekend, we began playing together. Steve's a great athlete, and I hadn't touched a racquet in 20 years. Still, often despite the heat, we'd play for two or three hours. I grew to love the game, and it came pretty naturally to me. Through tennis, Steve and I became very good friends.

When we would finish playing on hot days we'd go into the freezer and take out a huge jug of ice cold A & W Root Beer. We'd just sit there for an hour drinking the root beer and talking, and that's probably what solidified our friendship. Still, we had little idea we'd wind up going into practice together.

I also met Miles Berger for the first time at the post-camp. He and his wife, Sally, were seated at the same table with us. I had heard of Miles. He had been head of the Real Estate Planning Commission under the first Mayor Daley. He was obviously very smart, and a popular person in Chicago.

When they sat down at our table, Miles introduced himself and said, "I make the beds, my wife, Sally, is the athlete." Although he was joking, she was and is certainly quite a tennis player.

I shared office space with Miles for awhile and have been on the board of the Mid-Town Bank of Chicago for 23 years. Miles has served as chairman of the board and Joel Zemans is the president.

When Miles helped form the Mid-Town Bank, his accountant was a gentleman named Lester Rosenberg. He and his wife, Norma, are very good friends of ours and he is also on the board of the bank. At one point, Lester and I talked about merging our firms, but it never worked. There were just too many differences in the kinds of practices we had. Miles and Lester did, however, ask me if I wanted to be on the board and I gladly accepted. It has been a rewarding experience for me all around.

Anyway, for years I would drive up to Eagle River. I'd leave early in the morning, about 6 or 7, and try and to get up there for lunch. If I couldn't do that, I'd try to leave by 11:30 and get up there for dinner. I'll never forget one time, it was probably about 10:30 in the morning, and traffic was brutal. I must have been behind 20 cars, each one taking a long time to pass. This was the long stretch of two-lane highway, and I remember saying if I can just get going here, I could make lunch. Eventually, I passed all 20 cars, and as soon as I got past them, of course, there was nothing but open road ahead of me — and a policeman. It wasn't two minutes after I passed the last car that I got stopped for speeding somewhere past Sheboygan.

I told the policeman I'm guilty, I'll pay the ticket, I'll do anything, just let me out of here because I can't just sit here and watch all of these cars that it took me all this time to pass roll on by me. But I did. Eventually the driving just became really very tiresome and difficult. After a few years it became harder and harder for me to give up my Fridays. That's when I found a flight out of Meigs Field in Chicago, on a plane like the one that caused Leo Durocher such trouble years later.

There's been a lot of controversy in the last year or so as

to whether or not Meigs Field should stay open. It's on the lakefront right by the Field Museum, and it's about 10 minutes from my office. I would just grab a cab and fly out by 4:30 on Friday, and after a stop or two reach Eagle River around 6. Then I'd fly back on Monday morning, making it incredibly convenient.

My memories of all those summers revolve around friends, family and tennis. I remember my mother-in-law, Perle, who has unfortunately since passed away. She and I would play tennis against Ellen and her father, Al. Ellen's parents were both very good athletes, but their tennis games suffered because they spent the whole summer up there and didn't have too many people to play against.

When we played, I'd often find myself at the net. She'd be at the baseline and just in the middle of my overhead (I do have one) on a short lob, she'd yell, "Yours!" — as if it could have been anyone else's. But that was Perle, a strong and terrific woman.

A lot of people at the camp saw her as the boss. Al was smart enough to put her in charge of a lot of the many day-to-day things, but he and my brother-in-law Mickey truly ran the place.

I'm glad to have shared many a tennis game with Al and Perle because, emotionally and psychologically, it's the best sport for my temperament. I'm not long on patience, though I am a lot better than I used to be. I have played some golf, first when I was in the Navy. Not long after leaving the Navy, I played at the base in Glenview, Illinois, and shot an 82. That's a long way from what I'm shooting now.

But tennis is my game, and I'm getting better at it. I have been playing half my life. I've had an operation to remove some chips from my elbow and arthroscopes on both knees and my right wrist because years ago I tore ligaments in the wrist by opening a locker. In spite of it all, I'm now healthy and playing as much as I can.

One of my clients is Laura Pollack Fisher, who is now 92. She's the sister of Ferd Kramer, of Draper & Kramer. Ferd was a national tennis champion in the 70s, 80s and 90s age groups. He once told people he was having trouble moving and wasn't seeing very well. His doctors advised him not to play any more tennis. A short time later he won the nationals for those in their 90s. Someone asked how he was able to do that given his previous comments. He said, it was easy. I just changed doctors and had a cataract operation.

Laura is also quite a tennis player, but she is an even more amazing person with great charitable instincts. Not long ago I asked if she was still playing. She said she had no one to play with. I hope that doesn't happen to me. I'd like to play as long as I can.

It was at one of the post-camp sessions in Eagle River that I met Alan Schwartz, a great tennis player who was captain of Yale University's team. He was also, for a time, the doubles partner of Richard Raskin, who became more famous as Renee Richards.

Ellen and I were at Alan and his wife, Ronnie's, house for a dinner party the night before Renee Richards played her first professional match as a woman. I don't know why, but the evening was very strained, it was like a death watch. Ellen looked around at the silent faces and said, "So, what's new?" That seemed to break the tension.

I think Alan might have tried to become a professional tennis player if the money had been better in those days, but he was meant to be a very successful businessman. Amongst other things, he now owns and manages a chain of tennis courts and is the vice president and on the board of the United States Tennis Association (USTA). Coincidentally, we wound up being neighbors years later when we moved to the suburbs — our homes sat back-to-back.

I had been playing as much as I could, but the long days and cold winters didn't leave too much opportunity. One day, Alan gave me an application to an outdoor summer tennis club in Highland Park. Just fill this out, he said, it won't cost you anything to sign and you won't get in for another nine years. It did take nine years to get into the Birchwood Club, but it is without a doubt the best tennis club I've ever seen. It has four hard courts, twelve soft courts and is a great facility.

When I eventually started playing there, they had four or five teams, from A down to D or E. I was one of the better players on the B team, and in a few years joined the A team, which was kind of a thrill for me. I have a picture of me along with all the others, including a gentleman who was once the Big 10 champion and ranked in the top 10 in the U.S., and another gentleman who was a professional player in Europe. Through them, I've learned a lot about playing tennis.

Another good friend and regular partner of mine, Arnie Heltzer, also vacations with us down in Florida, where we play quite a bit. The first time I met Arnie, many years ago, we were to be playing the semifinals of a tournament in an indoor club in Highland Park. I got to the semis partly because someone defaulted and someone else got injured. I called Arnie and I asked when he wanted to play. He said, well, let's play according to my schedule because I'll be in the finals (which he was) and you won't, or something to that effect. That was Arnie, and still is. He's a great athlete, as is his wife, Gail, and they are both good friends of ours.

One day in Florida I was sitting on my second floor

balcony reading a book, and Arnie was standing more than two courts and two fences away. The next thing I know a ball comes over my balcony, over my book and into my lap. He couldn't do that again in a million years. Jerry Rotblatt was standing next to him and witnessed the whole thing. For Arnie's 55th birthday I put the autographed ball on a pedestal and gave it to him.

Arnie was usually Alan Schwartz's regular partner for Sunday morning matches. One day he was out of town, and I'm playing with Alan in Arnie's place and we're playing two fellows from some other club. Five doubles matches made up the schedule and it starts raining, and then starts raining harder. Everybody else walks off the court, but we're still out there. One of our opponents is serving, and it's really coming down, and he starts to leave the court. With that, Alan says it's up to the host of the club when you leave because of the rain, which of course isn't true. Then the man says, I can't do this. Alan says you can't stop on a serve, you have to finish the game once you start, which also isn't true. Finally, we won the game and, as we're walking off the court, Alan turns to me and says with a smile, it's really hard to serve in the rain.

As we're waiting in the club house for the rain to let up, Burt Ury, a good friend and truly wonderful and caring person, who is one of the owners of the Chicago Bulls and the White Sox and legendary captain of the 'A' team, notices the rain slow down, grabs a broom and heads out to the court to begin sweeping — while it's still raining.

I follow Burt out there and mention it's still raining out here. He looks at me with a straight face and says, "I'm doing everything I can, Harvey." He says what in the f___ do you want me to do? I said, well, if you're going to sweep, someone should at least try to get us some indoor courts. That's a great idea, he says, why don't you do that. So I got us indoor courts and we finished the matches.

As time went by, I went back to the B team, where I've played for a number of years. We did so well we just got moved up into the A league this year. So now we have two teams in the A league, and I'm proud to be the oldest player on either team. I owe this honor to my longtime partner and good friend, Jerry Rotblatt, who is a few years older than me and who decided he had had enough after all the years. It's a shame because I have made an exhaustive study of the entire country, and in addition to his many great character and other athletic skills, no one hits an overhead backhand like he does.

About 10 years ago, Ellen and I decided to try and find a way to break up the Chicago winters. We had visited some friends in Long Boat Key, which is on the west coast of Florida, about an hour south of Tampa. We liked it a lot, and I knew some people down there, including the Shimbergs, who were in Tampa. So, we looked around and ended up buying a condominium on the Gulf in one of five buildings that had eight hard tennis courts — which was like having the Birchwood of the South.

We've been there now for about 12 years, and it just gets better and better. The kids come down whenever they can get away, and everyone plays tennis. It's just been a wonderful experience. I've met a lot of fine people from many parts of the U.S. and Canada.

They have a Long Boat Key Club with tennis teams that play other clubs. The teams have age groups of 50s, 60s and 70s. When I turned 60, by then I had gotten to know everybody, I started playing for the 60 team and did pretty well. My second year there we won the league championship.

My playing kept getting interrupted, however, by various

surgeries. When I had wrist surgery I couldn't play for a couple of months, and it was suggested I try hitting left-handed. Well, I tried it for awhile and wound up learning a two-handed backhand, which is not quite lethal, but much more effective.

The Worldwide Maccabi Games are held every four years in Israel. They draw Jewish athletes from countries all over the world who compete in everything from track and baseball to soccer and tennis to volleyball, swimming and golf.

Every other year the Pan Am Maccabi Games are held, which is just for the Pan American part of the world — Canada, United States, Mexico, Central America and South America. I'd always wanted to play in those games, but never got the chance. In late 1995, Ellen and I went down to Buenos Aires, Argentina, which was where the games were being held. Now, in order to get into the Worldwide Maccabi Games in Israel you've got to go through all kinds of qualifying, but to get into the Pan Am Maccabi Games all you have to do is be willing to pay the fee, and show up, which I did.

I entered the 65-and-over masters division for tennis. Unfortunately, there weren't very many 65-and-over players, so I ended up playing in the 60-and-over division, where there were some better players. I won two silver medals, one in singles and one in doubles. My partner, Aaron Cushman, and I beat the number one seed in the semifinals, but lost in the finals, which got us a silver medal. In the singles I won four matches — I beat someone from Mexico and someone from Brazil — and lost two. The way the rounds were set up, I won a Silver there also.

The first match I lost was to a fellow from San Francisco who owns part of the San Francisco Giants and who was Alan Schwartz's partner when they won the gold medal in Israel in doubles. Now, Argentina in January is sweltering, and the red clay makes the points longer, but I certainly had no excuses. He won the first set, I won the second and I think I was winning the third when I just fell apart and lost 6-3 or 6-4. Ellen came on the court afterwards, and for the first time in my life I could barely get up. I was that exhausted. I didn't realize the water you drink during the match isn't as important as the water you drink before the match. Still, he beat me fair and square, and I wondered how I was going to get through nine more days of this. With the help of a good massage therapist at the Sheraton Hotel, and my own determination, I was proud of the way I finished.

Buenos Aires is a magnificent city. Despite riding a lot of buses, which made me feel like I was in the minor leagues, it was an exhilarating experience that I wouldn't trade for anything.

About eight years ago I was at a charity dinner and a woman named Sylvia Margulies came up to me and said, "Are you Harvey Wineberg?" She said she needed to have lunch with me to talk about something. I asked what and she said, why don't we just have lunch.

So we did, and Sylvia, who is very involved in almost every charitable activity in Chicago, told me she was working full time for the Cystic Fibrosis Foundation. One of her main events of the year was a Tennis Ball out in the suburbs, and she wanted to implement another one in the city. She told me I was referred to her as someone who might be willing to chair the first event of that kind.

I agreed to give it a try and, at first, wasn't so sure that I had made the right decision. It's not easy to get these events off the ground when there's no history to them. But one of my best attributes, I like to think, is surrounding yourself with good, smart people.

For this event, I called in a half dozen people I knew and said, look, you've got to help me with this. One of those people was Mike Barr, whom I met at the Birchwood Club and who was the previously mentioned European pro who also won national singles and doubles titles at both 35 and 40. So I asked Mike if he'd be on the committee because he's not only the best player I know, but he knows more about tennis than anybody I know. When Mike says he'll do something, he does it, so I was relieved when he agreed to help.

Shortly thereafter, Mike was playing golf with the head of Cellular One in Chicago. He convinced the man that his company needed to sponsor a charity like this and Cellular One became our sponsor. All the help I got from people like him made it a very special event. We raised more money than any first-time event Cystic Fibrosis ever had, and from there it just continued to grow.

The set-up involved 24 amateur men and 24 local tennis pros, four or six amateur women and four or six local tennis pro women. We would play in five flights, and the winners would play for first and through fifth. My partner Steve won the whole thing one year. My best finish was sixth.

Of all the Cystic Fibrosis tournaments I played in, I remember one in particular. We were at the event's black-tie dinner the night before and Shelley Fink was sitting at a table with the tennis pro Tim Gullikson and his wife, Rosemary, who was a lawyer at Shelley's firm. When I found out that Tim was going to play as Shelley's partner the next day, I walked around the room threatening to sue. This is absolutely unconscionable and illegal, I kiddingly ranted, since all we ever had were local pros. Rosemary enjoyed the joke and said, I think you're absolutely right, Harvey. "I'm going to sue

Shelley and my husband."

Tim Gullikson, as you may know, was Pete Sampras' coach. Tim's twin brother Tom is also a pro, and is now coach of the U.S. Davis Cup team. Tragically, Tim died of brain cancer more than a year ago after a long and courageous fight.

Ironically, that next day, when Tim played with Shelley, my partner and I ended up playing against them. They seemed to bring out the best in me, because that day I played better than I'm able.

Afterwards, Tim came up to me and said, you played better against me than anybody else here. I said, that's very nice of you, and on behalf of the other 20 or 30 people you've said that to, I thank you. He was a terrific person, and through Shelley he later sent me an autographed picture of him taken at Wimbledon with the Duke and the Duchess. On the bottom of the picture, he wrote: "To Harvey Wineberg, the man with the best forehand around."

His death was, of course, awfully sad. I've spent some time working with Rosemary, and she's a terrific person who's carrying on with great courage.

Last year was the eighth and final year of the tournament. Although the gene that causes cystic fibrosis has been isolated, the organization still needs financial support. But the event had successfully run its course. The organization is now looking into other fund-raising efforts.

Another charity I volunteered some time with was Columbus Hospital, where I was on the finance committee of the Columbus Hospital Foundation board. I had two runs at that, neither of which were overly rewarding. I did it because I wanted to do something for Dr. Len Cerullo and all of his people. I did make what I thought were meaningful contributions, but it's hard for a Jewish person from the suburbs to raise money for a Catholic hospital in Chicago. I did my best and served on the committee that headed up the last fund-raising event at the Field Museum.

At the moment, the charity part of my life seems to be in a lull, but I still keep busy with politics. Politics has been kind of the second love of my life. In the early years of my youth, I spent a lot of time in independent politics. I was one of the first supporters of, and the treasurer for, Bill Singer when he was an independent candidate against the first Mayor Daley — in the days when that wasn't such an easy or popular thing to do. Bill is now a successful lawyer and we still represent him.

Bill headed the original Chicago Cable Commission, on which I served. I believe we made a good start at bringing quality and affordable cable service to the people of Chicago.

I also represent Marty Oberman. Marty was a Chicago alderman and now heads the Chicago Council for Lawyers and is a practicing attorney. Marty made a couple of runs for attorney general that I helped with.

In the 1960s, I led a young splinter group called Voters for Peace. I marched in both New York and Washington and, while I was around during the 1968 riots, I managed to avoid the eye of the storm. The events of that day have obviously left a stain on the American psyche.

I could never understand why so many intelligent people could not see the tragedy that was building up in Vietnam. It seemed obvious our military was there for all the wrong reasons, and it didn't take much to see we were never going to return with any type of victory.

Years later, Harold Washington made history as the first black man to be elected mayor of Chicago. I am proud to have been involved in his campaign. He was the guest speaker at one of the ACLU dinners while I was the president. We sat together, and he was a most charming man. He had been a U.S. representative in Washington and was well-loved among most Chicagoans.

I'm currently the head of the nominating committee, which elects the board and the officers for the ACLU. One of the people on the board with me many years ago was Dawn Clark Netsch. I was the treasurer of her successful campaign for comptroller of the State of Illinois.

I remember one day Dawn and I were sitting next to each other in an ACLU board meeting. Some of the people there are prone, as well-intentioned as they may be, to argue over how many people can dance on the head of a pin. During this meeting, there was a long debate going on that had lost peoples' interest. As this went on, Dawn finally looked at me and said, "Harvey, I've got a feeling this one is about over, so we just have to get through a few more minutes." I said, "Dawn, I've got a feeling there's going to be a tie vote." Sure enough, they voted 22 to 22. Dawn and I both had one of many good laughs.

After Dawn's campaign, I joined my daughter Julie in working for Michael Dukakis. As a Democratic supporter, I had previously worked on George McGovern's and Jimmy Carter's campaigns for the presidency.

McGovern may or may not have made a good president, but I personally had a lot of respect for him. I thought he understood the problems of this country pretty well. There was quite a bit of clamoring about estate taxes being raised under McGovern and how he'd be taking money from the next generation. At one point, I had heard enough. In my opinion, the man's platform was to put our tax money to good use for the country as a whole. I saw nothing wrong with that.

In fact, it seemed downright obvious that we needed to take action rather than fear it. So I took a quarter page ad out in the *Chicago Tribune* expressing just how I felt. It read:

■ ■ ■

I want to leave
everything I can
to my children

That includes
a better world.

I will vote for
George McGovern.

Harvey Wineberg

■ ■ ■

Newsweek was among the publications that called me wanting to know who I was and what inspired my public and political display. I told them the ad spoke for itself.

As an active supporter of the Carter campaign, I once attended a fund-raising event for Carter's vice-presidential selection, Walter Mondale. It was a held at a magnificent home on Lake Michigan in Evanston. I remember walking in, and Walter Mondale's wife, Eleanor, was at the door greeting people. We were introduced, and I said I was really sorry that I hadn't met her sooner. She asked why, and I said because then I probably would have been vice-president of the United States. She loved that.

Later on in the evening, Walter Mondale spoke and — you have to picture this — the house right on Lake Michigan, a beautiful day, a magnificent home. He said to the group, President Carter and I have spent endless hours and days wondering whether or not we were providing the people of this country with adequate housing. He said, apparently we are.

From there I chose to work on behalf of the politician I was closest to, U.S. Senator Paul Simon, who was doing a magnificent job in my view. My daughter, Julie, made such a good impression with her work on the Dukakis campaign, that she was welcomed onto the Simon team.

I have always had great respect for Paul Simon. He's an honest, honorable, intelligent person, and I was honored to have spent a number of years working on his behalf.

During his last run for senator he called me and said, Harvey, I need a major fund-raising event in Chicago, and I'd like you to be the chairman of that committee. I told him, I'm probably the wrong person for the job. I also told him I wasn't a "big type" hitter in this town, that I can't pick up the phone and call in a lot of chips and expect a lot of people to come, bring friends and donate big money. He said, Harvey, I'm not looking for the big hitters in town. I want someone who will get the job done. That compliment won me over and we had a magnificent event at the Palmer House which raised a lot of money.

Although I'd like to take the credit for its success, we were lucky enough to get Harry Belafonte and Peter Yarrow of Peter, Paul & Mary for the evening's entertainment. They put on such a wonderful show we actually taped it and sent it out to other places for their events.

I was sorry when Paul decided not to run again, but fortunately he endorsed a man who, although I had not known well, I also had a great deal of respect for, Dick Durbin. Durbin took Simon's Senate seat in 1996.

While I was doing some work for Durbin and raising some money, we were advised that anyone who had raised X amount of dollars would be invited to a somewhat semi-private gathering with Durbin and President Clinton, who was in town to support Durbin. On the same night as this event, my oldest daughter, Susan, went to the hospital to deliver her second son. We told some people that we had to get over to the hospital, and they pushed us toward the front of the line. Ellen and I went up and had our picture taken with President Clinton and Senator Durbin. Ellen told the president not to worry about a thing. "There aren't enough open-neck sport shirts in the country for Senator Dole to beat you," she said.

"I'd like to talk to you longer," I told the president, "but my oldest daughter is delivering a baby." He asked if this was her first and I told him it was her second. He said, well, wish her good luck. I promised him we would and then wished him good luck. We shook hands and left, and later on we received a colored photo, which is an exciting momento to have.

I was literally amazed by the magnetism and the energy that Clinton exudes. This was probably his fourth event of the day, I thought. He had to be dog tired because it was also nearing the end of the campaign. But he just stood there meeting people, and could not have been more charming.

Whether you agree with Clinton on everything or not, you'd have to concede that he is one master politician. Some of us who have been somewhat disillusioned with a lot of things that have happened over the last few years like to say he may not be perfect, but he is our less-than-perfect president.

Obviously, the country has never been better economically, and I believe he has strong and passionate concerns, as do I, on important issues like pro-choice, gay rights, gun control, affirmative action and other social issues.

CHAPTER X
Good Sports and Great Clients

It was 1993, in Phoenix, with the Bulls leading the series with the Suns three games to two — but struggling — when he hit "The Shot." As every Bulls' fan knows, it was not only the game winner, but the shot that clinched the team's third NBA Championship.

No, it wasn't Michael Jordan. It was John Paxson, who is as great a person as he was a basketball player. I've had the pleasure of working with John, and am proud to call him a good friend. John, his wife, Carolyn, and sons, Ryan and Drew, live near us in a neighboring northern suburb. Over the years, our families have become close, and I continue to work with John on his post-basketball business affairs.

It all started years ago with his older brother Jim, who also played in the NBA for years. Jim was an all-star with the

Portland Trailblazers before finishing his career in Boston. Our firm represented Jim for a long time. He was the beneficiary of one of the first significant NBA contracts, but shortly thereafter we had a difference of opinion with Jim on what financial approach he ought to take from there.

He met some financial people out in Los Angeles, who, I believe, took a very conservative approach. We thought he was too young for that and, after a while, Jim wound up using them instead. Despite our parting of ways, Jim is a terrific person. He is now an assistant general manager with Portland. He and John remain very close.

Because of our history with Jim, I was surprised when we got a call from John saying his brother suggested he give us a call. John was still at Notre Dame University at the time, so we agreed to meet with him when he came to town for an upcoming game with DePaul University at the Rosemont Horizon in suburban Chicago. Steve and I waited for John after the game. We knew he was going to be a high draft choice, and we were impressed with him — and I guess he with us — so we agreed to handle all of his financial affairs.

Although he ended his career with the Bulls and will forever be remembered as a local hero, there was at one point a good chance that John might miss the team's championship ride.

John was drafted by San Antonio and spent a couple of mediocre seasons with the Spurs before he was traded to the Chicago Bulls. John wasn't much older than my daughter, Susan, but we became very close. He and Carolyn would come to our house and just relax, chat and gossip. I can't say that I've ever known a nicer young couple.

Since he wasn't a major force in the NBA, John handled his own contract negotiations in the beginning of his career.

He never felt he had the leverage to have an agent act as his representative. For a time, he was the lowest paid starting guard in the NBA. To the Bulls and owner Jerry Reinsdorf's credit, they did something about that when they could, which John always appreciated.

As John neared the end of his contract during the 1990-1991 season, he asked me if I would talk to Reinsdorf and Bulls' general manager Jerry Krause about his next contract. He knew we didn't negotiate contracts anymore, that we focused on financial management, but as a favor — and because I knew both Reinsdorf and Krause — I told John I would talk to them.

I met with the two Jerry's, as they are sometimes called, to discuss John's situation. Krause pretty much had his mind made up that 32-year-old guards, for the most part, are not able to compete effectively much longer in the NBA. There were several exceptions to that rule, but his bottom line was simple, and the team offered a modest increase over two years.

Obviously, we wanted a much larger increase, and we wanted it for three years. I told John that I didn't think there was any point in taking this any further, we weren't likely to get what we wanted with the Bulls — even though John very much wanted to stay in Chicago.

John had had great success as a Bull up to that point. He knew the system well and fit into it perfectly. Playing with Michael Jordan wasn't so bad either. Still, I suggested we forget about the contract, concentrate on finishing the season strongly and then see what offers were out there as a free agent. Ultimately, I said, I think the Bulls want to keep you. That's the way we left it.

Coincidentally, Jerry Reinsdorf called not long after that and said, Harvey, I really think that John needs some leverage that he doesn't have right now. Reinsdorf repeated what I had said to John about concerning himself with having a productive season and, hopefully, a solid post-season. He said we'll talk at the end of the season when John might have more leverage and better options.

As fate and luck would have it, the Bulls glided through the playoffs and into the championship series with the Los Angeles Lakers. John came up big throughout the series and hit five baskets down the stretch that set up the team's first NBA title. With that game, he became one of the heroes, and clearly proved his worth to the team and its owners.

Shortly after that career-making game, Michael Jordan talked to John about his status and suggested that John use his agent, David Falk, for the simple reason that it would offer John better positioning. John mentioned this to me, and I said by all means use Falk. All I care about is that you get the best possible deal for yourself. He did go with Falk.

I've met David and have great respect for him. This gave John even more leverage. Plus, San Antonio wanted him back, and the Bulls wanted to keep him. John got a very good contract. I don't think it was anything I couldn't have secured as well, but it certainly worked out and everyone was happy.

It was not only thoughtful, but smart for Jordan to show concern for John's situation. Like most people, I am a huge Michael Jordan basketball fan. I am not, however, as huge a fan of Michael Jordan the person. But I am able to separate the two.

Having gotten to know hundreds of athletes over the years, I've found that some of them are fabulous athletes and fabulous people. Others are good athletes but not such good people. I think the pressures on Michael Jordan have to be almost unimaginable. I also think, however, that Jordan tends to be a bit too image-conscious, and that that keeps him from taking a stance on issues of the day. At his level of notoriety and with his lack of any normal semblance of life, he has good reason to shield himself from public debate, but I think he is in a position to do more than he probably does for a lot of very good causes. I know he has his own foundation, to which he contributes some of his earnings, but I think he has to let people know that he's living for more than just being the most famous person in the world, the greatest basketball player ever and someone who makes millions from endorsing everything from perfume to pick-up trucks.

In reading Arthur Ashe's book, *Days of Grace* (Knopf) — which he finished shortly before he died — I was struck by his account of Jordan's rather extreme lack of political responsibility. Ashe wrote:

■ ■ ■

> ...While I would defend Jordan's right to stay out of politics in general, I think that he made a mistake in declining to give any open support to Harvey Gantt, the respected black politician who ran for the U.S. Senate in 1990 from Jordan's home state of North Carolina. For me, the main point is not that Gantt and Jordan are both black; rather, it is that Gantt's opponent, Jesse Helms, has a long history of supporting segregation, and the contest was close. For blacks across America, that Senate contest was the most important in decades. Instead, Jordan stuck to his apolitical position. 'I don't really know Gantt,' he said, in response to criticism of his silence. 'Well, Michael,' I would have told him, 'pick up the telephone and call him!' A few appearances with Gantt might well have made the difference. Instead, Helms returned to the Senate.

That's an example of some obligations that I don't think Jordan fully honors, but he certainly has a lot of time to correct that. In the meantime, I will continue to enjoy this basketball phenomenon. For those who aren't able to watch him every night like we do here in Chicago, it's almost beyond description. I have never seen anybody — in any phase of sports, entertainment, business or anything else — who can perform night in and night out at the level he does. He is truly one-of-a-kind.

With the new contract, John Paxson figured he was going to be here for awhile. He had his eye on a new home and asked me if he could really afford to buy the house. I told him, John, at the end of this contract you will be financially secure, so don't worry about it. He bought the house, and little did we both realize how right I was.

In the meantime, the Bulls again outplayed the competition and found themselves facing Charles Barkley and the Phoenix Suns in the 1993 championship series. With the Bulls looking sluggish, and Barkley seeming to get stronger, the team was in dire need of a spark. The Bulls got the ball back with about ten seconds left, down by two. As the clock wound down, the ball went inside to Horace Grant, who passed it out to Paxson just beyond the three-point line. Although the Suns got one last chance, Grant blocked the attempt. "The Shot" won the championship, number three.

When John came back to town the next night he had yet to sleep — either because he was out celebrating or too wired. He called and asked if Ellen and I wanted to come over. Of course we did. When we got there he was on a natural high, but perhaps not as fired up as his son, Drew, who was just three-and-a-half at the time. John had nailed a basketball hoop and backboard low on a tree, and Drew challenged me to a game. He took three alternate shots and made them all, and I took two shots and made them both. Then he grabbed the ball and said, "I won three to two." I said, no, you didn't win. You went first, so I get another shot. Drew looked me right in the eye and said, "I have no idea what you're talking about." He'll be a star in whatever he does.

And Ryan, he's going to be an NBA player if I ever saw one. He's not only a great shooter and rebounder, he's a fierce competitor. Now 10-years-old, Ryan is already the three-point champ of Lake Bluff.

I went to a game of his and I'm sitting there next to John, Carolyn and Drew, and with about 15 seconds to go in the game and his team losing by one point, Ryan gets the ball from out of bounds and dribbles down the court. Like any other father and fan, John yells with about five seconds to go for Ryan to shoot. Ryan passes off to someone else, and John smacks himself in the forehead in dismay. Ryan runs toward the corner and with two seconds to go the ball gets passed back to Ryan, who lets it go from the corner just before the buzzer.

Of course, the ball goes in and Ryan's team wins. I look at John and say, "I think I've seen all this before." John smiles and says, he's better than I was at that age.

After John retired from the game, I negotiated a contract for him to do radio broadcasting with the Bulls alongside Neil Funk. He then spent a year as assistant coach to Phil Jackson, a man he holds in high regard, but after that season he promised himself and his family that he'd take some time off before getting caught up in another whirlwind year of professional basketball. That year is now up and we just finished his contract to do television color commentary for all the Bulls' games on WGN-TV and Sports Channel.

As busy as John has been in his basketball life, he's always found time to do what he can to help others. My daughter Margi's summer camp is a perfect example of this. Margi is a social worker, and in the summer she runs a camp called TWIG (Together We Influence Growth) at a grammar school in Winnetka, a North Shore suburb. After starting out as a counselor, Margi became director of the camp several years ago. Half of the children are from the North Shore, and half come from the inner city, so it's basically half white, half black. When John heard about the camp he offered his help; she didn't even have to ask.

Almost every year John gives Margi a call and sets up a visit to the camp. It's just the most exciting thing for these kids when he drops by and talks to the them about basketball and about life. He always does a little dribbling lesson and works with them on shooting, and I think he has as much fun as they do. That's just the kind of person he is.

Over the years, we've represented other NBA players, including a man named Delaney Rudd. Rudd served as back-up to John Stockton in Utah for a couple seasons and is now a basketball star in France.

We've been representing Orlando Woolridge ever since he graduated from Notre Dame. I remember flying down to Shreveport, Louisiana, to meet him and his father. I get off the plane, and there are two of the longest Cadillacs I've ever seen. Orlando gets out of one, and his dad gets out of the other. I say to myself, I think there's a problem here.

Coincidentally, Orlando became a Chicago Bull. From the start we were trying to do our best to make sure Orlando did the right things. His father wasn't always appreciative, and at one point I sent him an airline ticket and said you'd better get up to Chicago so we can talk before this relationship gets any worse. He came up and joined me, my partner Steve and Orlando for a meeting. I looked at his father and basically said, one of the great things in this world, Mr. Woolridge, is that no one really needs anyone else. You don't need me, and I don't need you. Either we're going to do this the way we think is right, or we're not going to do it at all.

We're still representing Orlando, although he has had his share of troubles over the years. After a number of years in the NBA, he played over in Europe. It's no secret that at one point he had a drug problem. When he got out of rehabilitation he called me and thanked me for all the concern I showed. I think that's probably part of the recommended treatment, to acknowledge those who have tried to help you. That was when I was more involved with him. Steve has really handled the relationship recently and has gone way beyond the call of service. Orlando is now coaching in the new professional women's basketball league.

Bill Laimbeer, Orlando's teammate at Notre Dame, is another story. Unlike Orlando, Bill was never really thought of as superstar potential — certainly not at Notre Dame, where they also had players like Kelly Tripucka and others at the time.

Bill spent his first two years with the Cleveland Cavaliers, who didn't seem too high on him either because he was traded to Detroit. It was, of course, as a Piston that Bill made a name for himself. Beloved in Detroit for the fierce style of play that helped bring two NBA championships to the city, Bill wasn't so well-liked in other NBA cities. He was the kind of player that if he's on the other team, you hate him, but if he's on your team, you love him.

People think Bill's difficult, and he may be, but we've not had a minute of trouble from him. His philosophy is that I'm going to take care of my family, and I'm going to take care of my team, and anybody who gets in the way better look out. I don't think most people could comfortably take that attitude, but Bill sure has. He has a beautiful family to look out for, a wonderful wife, Kris, and two great young kids. His passion and determination has allowed him to succeed in everything he's done. Since retiring, Bill has joined his father in their own packaging company. Interestingly, in a recent interview he admitted that he needs to mellow out a little, and I'm sure he will.

When Bill's jersey was retired in Detroit, Steve and I flew up for the ceremony at the Palace. We went to dinner afterward and I was talking to his dad, who said we really need to talk about estate planning for Bill. Then, he said, Harvey, you should know that as far as I'm concerned my idea of perfect estate planning is having the check to the funeral home bounce. That was his way of saying that by the time you die everything you have is either given away, put into trusts or handled properly enough so there's no estate tax to pay. It seems the apple hasn't fallen far in the case of Bill Laimbeer, and it's been quite a pleasant experience getting to know him and his family.

Two other basketball men who I greatly admired are Dean Smith and Jim Valvano. I met both of them at different times through Jack Marin. Jack had been trying to develop a relationship with them hoping that the combination of his services as an agent and Steve and me as financial managers would be a selling point for both coaches, or that at least they would encourage their graduating players to consider Jack as an agent without automatically going to the so-called big boys.

The difference between Dean Smith and Jim Valvano is like night and day. Dean Smith, of course, recently retired as the winningest college coach in history. He is a legend in his own time. I went down to North Carolina and, along with Jack, had a chance to speak with him for awhile. He couldn't have been more charming. He's a real gentleman.

At some point the subject of politics came up, and he looked at Jack and me and said, don't talk to me about who's going to win in politics. He said, I voted for George McGovern, which kind of shocked me, and I said I too voted for George McGovern, but I didn't think anybody in sports did, and I certainly didn't think anybody in North Carolina did. And Dean said, well, that means we must be the only two people standing in the state of North Carolina right now who voted for George McGovern, and he laughed.

Jim Valvano was a far different person than Dean Smith. When I visited him for the first time, his secretary walked me into his office and he was standing in his warm-up suit. I introduced myself, and instead of saying hello, he said, who's the best defensive coach in college basketball? I had heard that one before but said, I don't know, but if you want me to say you, I'd be glad to. He said, no, Dean Smith is the best defensive coach in college basketball — him not knowing, of course, that I was a great admirer of Dean Smith. And he added, you tell me who else could hold Michael Jordan, James Worthy, Sam Perkins and the rest of those guys to 65 points a game.

That was obviously Valvano's way of stoking the fire between his intra-state rival. It was no secret, however, how much respect Valvano had for Dean Smith. Valvano was just a very funny man. At one point he jumped up on his secretary's desk, a lady whom I'm sure had seen these antics before, and said, do you know over at Georgia Tech the only food you can bring into the athletic department building is one piece of fruit? He looks at her and says, tell me, if you're bringing in a bunch of grapes, is that one fruit or more than one fruit? She finally convinced him to get off her desk, and we continued our conversation. Amazed by this man's energy and lightning quick wit, at the end of our meeting I told him he ought to run for public office. He looked at me like I had lost my mind.

Jim Valvano died way before his time. I'll never forget the year North Carolina State won the NCAA tournament. I remember him jumping 20 feet off the floor. That said it all.

When he was alive, Valvano liked to give people a copy of "The Station," an inspirational writing by Robert Hastings. He gave me a copy as well.

■ ■ ■

THE STATION
By Robert Hastings

Tucked away in our subconscious is an idyllic vision. We see ourselves on a long trip that spans the continent. We are traveling by train. Out the windows we drink in the passing scene of cars on nearby highways, of children waving at a crossing, of cattle grazing on a distant hillside, of smoke pouring from a power plant, of row upon row of corn and wheat, of flatlands and valleys, of mountains and rolling hillsides, of city skylines and village halls.

But uppermost in our minds is the final destination. On a certain day at a certain hour we will pull into the station. Bands will be playing and flags waving. Once we get there so many wonderful dreams will come true and the pieces of our lives will fit together like a completed jigsaw puzzle. How restlessly we pace the aisles, damning the minutes for loitering — waiting, waiting, waiting for the station.

'When we reach the station, that will be it!' we cry. 'When I'm 18.' 'When I buy a new 450 SL Mercedes Benz!' 'When I put the last kid through college.' 'When I have paid off the mortgage!' 'When I get a promotion.' 'When I reach the age of retirement, I shall live happily ever after!'

Sooner or later we must realize there is no station, no one place to arrive at once and for all. The true joy of life is the trip. The station is only a dream. It constantly outdistances us.

'Relish the moment' is a good motto, especially coupled with Psalm 118:24: 'This is the day which the Lord hath made; we will rejoice and be glad in it.' It isn't the burdens of today that drive men mad. It is the regrets over yesterday and the fear of tomorrow. Regret and fear are twin thieves who rob us of today.

So stop pacing the aisles and counting the miles. Instead, climb more mountains, eat more ice cream, go barefoot more often, swim more rivers, watch more sunsets, laugh more, cry less. Life must be lived as we go along. The station will come soon enough.

■ ■ ■

I think Valvano truly lived his life by this creed. For one who left too soon, he lived as full a life as he could have.

From a business standpoint, my dealings with both Valvano and Dean Smith were not productive. The bottom line with coaches like them is that the relationships they form with those they deal with are so strong that they're hard to break. I think they feel an obligation to make sure their superstars are represented by people with long-time reputations, so that if anything goes wrong, at least they can't be accused of taking chances. One of the problems in the business is its tendency to perpetuate itself. You've got some super powerful agents and it's hard for even the brightest young men like Jack Marin and others to break into that business. Still, Jack has done very well.

We continued to succeed as well. Although our work with professional football players was limited, we did have the opportunity to represent Willie Gault, the noted wide receiver for the Bears and later the Raiders.

Willie was active in the Better Boys Foundation, and that's how we met him. (In fact, we just recently started working with Joe and Lou Anne Kellman, who are greatly responsible for the fine work that organization does and are also involved with many other charities.) For a few years, we handled everything we could for Willie. When he left Chicago for the Raiders, he chose to work with a West Coast firm with ties to the film industry. The only sad experience we had with Willie was his not being able to fulfill his and his wife's dream of successfully running an avant garde men's and women's clothing store.

I literally begged Willie not to do it. First of all, the mortality rate in that business is high, and, secondly, he wasn't going to be around long enough to see it through. But Willie actually set it up without even telling us, and he set it up the wrong way so that we weren't able to take advantage of the initial year losses, losses that are not uncommon in any business. His store location was also questionable, and it just didn't work.

There's no polite way of telling someone they made a mistake and that they should consider taking other peoples' advice. Still, we left on good terms. Willie was and is a terrific athlete. With his ambition, I'm sure he and his family are doing well in California, where he's now an actor.

We also worked with a couple of soccer players. Derek Spalding was a defender for the Chicago Sting during the years they won the league title. My daughter, Margi, and I went up to Toronto to see them win the Soccer Bowl in 1981. Derek was a good friend, and we were with him for a long time. I negotiated a contract for Derek with Willie Roy, who at that time was the coach and general manager of the Chicago Sting. The team's owner was Lee Stern, a gentleman I know pretty well and whose wife, Norma, was a high school friend of mine.

In those days, soccer hadn't really caught on, and I guess it still hasn't, but it was even tougher then, and the money wasn't being thrown around very freely. Even though Derek was one of the stars and a captain of the team, the organization was giving us a tough time. Finally, after a lot of really tough negotiations, I worked out an agreement with Willie Roy that we had shaken hands on and were supposed to sign. The next thing I know, he was vetoed, even though he clearly had the authority to make the deal. That left a bad taste in my mouth. Maybe that's the way they did things in the soccer league, but it wasn't right then, and it wouldn't be right now.

We also did some work for world-class soccer player Arno Steffenhagen, but we haven't been involved in soccer for a long, long time. It's a strange situation. I remember when everyone would say as soon as the kids start playing soccer, ten years later the crowds will be there. Well, they are still playing it, and love it, but for some reason it hasn't translated into the professional audience. Although it's an exciting game once you understand it, my own feeling is it probably never will draw the masses. It just isn't our game any more than baseball, basketball and football are someone else's game.

In addition to the athletes, I've been fortunate enough to have developed a practice that is just perfect for me. I've always told my kids and I've always believed that if you do something that you like, you will not only do it well, but you will enjoy it even more. I've been lucky enough to do that.

I feel as if I'm part financial therapist and part good friend. Over the years, we've built a practice on that philosophy. We now have eight CPAs and five support staff. We do more than 1,400 tax returns of one kind or another for individuals, corporations, partnerships, trusts, pensions, foundations, etc.

Steve Lewis and I have been together for 25 years. It's been a spectacular experience. During all of those years, we've had just one serious disagreement, but we were smart enough to work it out. We have been able to attract clients who believed in us and knew that we cared. That's been a credit to everyone who has worked with us and for us.

We've been representing the great jazz pianist Ramsey Lewis for several years. He is a true gentleman and good friend. He's had good times and bad, and we've tried to be there when he's needed us. He has seven children, he has gotten divorced and he is now married to his present wife, Jan, who is terrific. Ramsey's been to all of my daughters' weddings, and I went to his father's funeral, which I'll never forget. I love gospel music, and the funeral was filled with it. Although it may seem strange to say, I didn't want the funeral to end, the music was that great.

Some other entertainment figures we've worked with have included Chicago radio personalities Steve Dahl and Gary Meier. We represented them for 10 years when they were an on-air team, and we still work with Gary.

When I was representing Steve and Gary in negotiations for their contracts with WLUP radio in Chicago, the person

I was up against was Jimmy DeCastro, president of the "Loop," as the station is called. DeCastro formed a larger company called Evergreen Media (now Chancellor Media). He was very impressed with the way we handled things, and asked if we'd represent him. I said, well, if Steve and Gary don't think there's a conflict, we'd love to. They didn't and we've been working with Jimmy for years.

Jimmy is a dynamo, certainly the leading young player in his field. His company has been buying and selling other companies, and now they're all over the country. Jimmy's a busy man. I don't sit down for very long, but he sits down even less.

We represented Chicago Cubs' broadcaster Harry Caray for a few years, but a difference of opinion proved irreconcilable. I felt bad about it, but since I felt I had no choice, I have no regrets. Like the rest of Chicago, I'll miss him.

I've been really fortunate in not knowing what comes first, the chicken or the egg. Almost all of my good friends are clients, and almost all of my clients are good friends. Dr. Leonard Cerullo, who I've already mentioned, is one person who fits into that category. He loves people and they love him back. Len has developed an excellent neurosurgical program for brains and backs at Columbus Hospital utilizing the only Gamma Knife (non-invasive) in the midwest. The biggest compliment I can pay him is that, God forbid I should ever have a brain or back problem of any seriousness, he'd be the only person I'd go to. I personally know what he's done for so many.

Some other noteworthy clients over the years have included a gentleman named Jack Goeken, who started MCI in his garage and saw it grow into what it is today. He's one of those people with a brilliantly creative mind. He was the original founder of Air Fone. When he sold out to GTE, according to newspaper reports, one of the provisions was that in addition to the buy out money, he would receive an earn-out based on how successful Air Fone was.

It's not uncommon to have an earn-out on the sale of a business, but one day Jack stopped in my office and, after he told me his joke of the week, said, Harvey, the man they hired at Air Fone doesn't know what he's doing, and it's affecting my earn-out. I think that I ought to sue them, he said, and I was wondering how you feel about that. I said, well, I suppose if you could find a lawyer who will take it then do it, but it doesn't sound like a very strong case to me. I can't imagine that GTE went out and hired someone incompetent just to hurt you.

Nevertheless, he eventually found a major law firm in Chicago that thought he had a case. When they got this gentleman who was running the company on the witness stand, Jack's lawyer said to him, we've checked your background and can't see anything that shows you have the knowledge and experience to head up a company in the airline industry like this. Could you tell us, the attorney continued, why you feel you are an airline expert that would justify your being hired to run Air Fone? The man said, absolutely, I have a wealth of experience in the airline industry. They asked him what it was, and the man said he was a "frequent flyer." Whether it was because of that answer or not, Jack won his case — which proves that you never know in this world.

We also work with a number of real estate people, including John Buck, one of the leading developers in the city who is on the verge of a $550 million development on Michigan Avenue, featuring Nordstroms. We also do work for Goldie Wolfe, who used to be the top realtor at Arthur Rubloff and who has since started her own company. It would be wrong to say that she's the leading female realtor in Chicago, because she's the city's leading office realtor altogether.

As I said, we've done a lot of work for the Sonnenschein law firm and for many of the partners there. Sam Rosenthal, Bernie Nath and Leo Carlin were the three name partners and Donald Lubin was the managing partner for many years. Sam Rosenthal once asked me to do something for him, and I said, what do you want me to charge you for this? He said, whatever you think, Harvey. I never argue about professional fees, he said. If I have confidence in the people, then I pay them what they tell me their job was worth. I've always tried to remember that. I don't know if everyone would agree with it, but I think it's not a bad way to live. He felt he trusted his advisors.

Besides Dr. Cerullo, the other surgeon I've spent a lot of time with and have great respect for is Dr. Bob Replogle, a world-famous heart surgeon. I've worked closely with him and his wife, Carol, who is a Ph.D. in her own right in English literature at Loyola University. Bob was at Michael Reese Hospital and is now at Ingalls Hospital. He's also the past president of the Society of Thoracic Surgeons, which has kept him traveling all over the world. He is really trying to do something about the health care problems that face the world today, and he's smart enough to make a big difference.

I've had the pleasure of working with Al Schreisheim, who was the executive director of Argonne National Laboratory; Lou Susman, who's the head of Salomon Brothers in Chicago; Jim Glasser, the retired chairman of the GATX Corporation; Ted Perlman, the head of the Havi Group, and his extended family; and Tom Pick and his extended family.

We've also worked with the Cooney family a lot. Bob

Cooney, Sr., died a few years ago; and we work with his sons, John and Bob Jr., of Cooney & Conway, an outstanding law firm. We also work with artists, from the well-known interior designer Bruce Gregga to the world-renowned fashion photographer Skrebneski.

Other special clients include Dick Stevens and Bob Long, developers and managers of the Yorktown Shopping Center; Lowell Stahl, the past president of Century 21 Central States; Mike McCarthy of Parkside Senior Services; and Aaron Cushman, President of Cushman and Associates. Years ago Aaron sent us an extra check saying he didn't think we were charging him enough for all we were doing. That's the only time that's happened to me and a great testimony to his character.

Bob Schrayer of Associated Insurance Agencies, whom I've not only represented, but been friends with for many years now, started out in his own agency and ended up buying Associated. When he bought the company, the bank said he needed a certified audit. Bob said, no I don't, Harvey's been good for me all these years, why would I need one, and why do I need another accounting firm in here?

Finally, I met with the banker and said, look, this isn't me talking. It's all right with me if you feel you have to have one. That's up to Bob. We'll still do the tax work. So, after a couple of years they ended up hiring a big firm to do the audit, and during their watch there was a major embezzlement, and to Bob's credit, he and his son, Skip, and his people saw it all through. I'm not sure I know anybody else who could have lived through it and come out so well. I remember telling Bob it probably wasn't worth the fight, but they managed to do it, and now we're back doing the accounting and the taxes.

Just a couple of months ago I told Bob if this would have

happened on our watch, even though it would never have been our fault because we didn't even do a certified audit, I would never have felt right, and you would never have felt right. I'm thankful that things turned out okay.

Other friends and clients who have been special in my life are Mort Kaplan and Heddy Ratner, Jim and Peggy Swartchild, Marcia Wagner and her late husband, Vern, and Dr. Elmer Kadison and his wife, Tedde.

The first time I played tennis with Mort Kaplan, which was before I became a better tennis player and he became a better golfer, we split sets. The next day he took an ad out in the *Chicago Tribune* which read, "Kaplan beats Wineberg 4-6, 6-4." Now that's a good public relations man. Our friendship with Jim and Peggy Swartchild has been a long one, and they've proven that good things happen to good people.

Marcia Wagner is my double cousin. Her father was my father's uncle and they married sisters. Her father was the youngest of eight Nierman children and my father's mother was the oldest of them. Sometimes it's not until later in life that we appreciate great friends and then wonder why it took so long.

Elmer Kadison is, quite simply, an amazing man. He took and passed the Florida boards at age 72, the oldest person in that state's history to do so. He is now doing neuro developmental evaluation of children aged four to fifteen for a Catholic church in Florida. He is truly a doctor's doctor.

Judy and Mickey Gaynor are also longtime friends, as are Larry and Doris Ashkin. Larry and I must have played tennis 30 times in the last five years, and I bet we've each won 15 sets.

Lucy and Ed Minor are extra special to me. Lucy has been my wife's best friend since we moved to the suburbs. Some people think they're sisters. They have this great capacity to be best friends without being constantly together and without intruding into each other's lives. They both know how to have the right kind of friendship.

Some years ago they decided they would write greeting cards for a company called California Dreamers. At their peak, things were very exciting, they were on the "Today Show" and "A.M. Chicago." They are both extremely clever and funny and quick with words, and I know they got a big kick out of doing it. Eventually, California Dreamers merged into or was sold to Recycled Paper Company, a company that didn't take such good care of their writers, which caused them to move on to other things.

Ed Minor has a very successful steel processing business. He had been in the steel and scrap business for years and then decided there was a need for a new type of steel processing, which he now does in his plants in East Chicago, Indiana, and Granite City, Illinois. Many years ago, when we first met, he asked what I would think about him being his company's accountant. I told him I didn't think that was a very good idea because he needed a bigger firm, one that would do certified audits. I also thought our relationship was too new to offer my firm's help. I didn't want to do anything that would jeopardize either his and my friendship or Ellen and Lucy's friendship.

A few years ago, he took me to lunch one day and said, if you bought steel and didn't buy from me, I'd be upset, and I have no idea why I'm not using you for my personal accounting. You're the trustee of all my trusts, and you're my confidante. So I became his accountant. The next year he was nice enough to call and tell me how thrilled he was to have made that move. I told him I was just as thrilled.

Allan and Elaine Muchin are a somewhat different story. We met a little bit later, and our children went to school together. Between us, the Muchins and the Minors, we have nine daughters, so there are many great common bonds between us. Elaine has a masters in social work and she and Lucy are the two closest women friends I have. Deep down we have the same feelings about what life should be about.

Allan Muchin is probably best known for having started a law firm from scratch with a few other partners, as well as being involved with many business and charity boards in the city. There's no doubt in my mind that Allan was and is the prime mover of the firm, which now has over 300 lawyers in offices throughout the country. We have been each others' trustee for years. More recently, I have become professionally involved with him and his friend Jerry Reinsdorf. It's an honor to work with them.

Years ago, Allan and I took an immediate liking to each other. Amongst many other things, we both have a strong interest in sports. We've played a lot of tennis together, and he would probably agree that now that he holds the extra ball in his left pocket, instead of his right, as soon as he just snaps his wrist a little more on his second serve, he'll be unbeatable.

Allan has as dry a sense of humor as anyone I know. If he didn't want to be a lawyer, he could have made a good living as a master of ceremonies. Having traveled with him and Elaine, the four of us have spent a lot of time together. We've been to Switzerland , France, Italy, Belgium, the Netherlands and Spain. Outside of the fact that they somehow seem to get the better room in most hotels, which I'm sure is pure coincidence, we get along famously. I remember in Switzerland somehow we took the wrong route, which meant going over the Alps instead of around them. I wasn't feeling great and Allan ended up doing the driving. Those roads in the mountains were not my favorite place, and I'm convinced that his driving saved my life a number of times.

Because of Allan, one of our newest and most prominent clients is Jerry Reinsdorf. Although Jerry and I have been on opposite sides of the negotiating table in the past, we agreed our representation of him would cause no real conflict of interest. When I asked if we could use his name in our client brochure, he said, sure, but he did suggest that it might be better if his and Bill Laimbeer's names not appear on the same page.

Jerry is an extremely intelligent and very strong person. As is the case with many of my clients, we may not always agree on everything, but how anyone could not think he is by far the top sports team owner in Chicago and one of the top owners nationally is beyond me. I don't think people realize how difficult it is to build, and then maintain, a winning franchise. There are many problems and personalities to manage, and he does it very well.

It is my partner, Steve Lewis, who has helped me climb the peaks of my professional career. He is as much like a son or brother to me as he is a business partner and friend. We've been together long enough that we think alike, and I guess act alike. He's been just a wonderful, loyal, dependable, honest and smart partner, and I hope he takes as much pride in all that we've been able to build and develop as I do. It was a great sense of fate and good luck that brought us together, and because I'm not planning on going anywhere for awhile, I trust that he and his wife, Melanie, will be close to us for many more years to come.

I hope that all of the other wonderful people in my office know how I feel about them; they are, after all, my second family. My secretary, Kris Schmidt, has been with me a long time and is much more than a secretary. She handles much of our financial matters and all of our tax returns, and she's very smart and very efficient. She's also done an incredible job raising two teenage sons.

Speaking of important people, I'd like to recognize the secretaries, administrative assistants, bookkeepers, etc., of the many companies we've worked with over the years. They have been so helpful. Their bosses may be important and powerful, but they are the ones who make it all work. So thanks to Camille, Geri, Carmella, Vonda, Debbie, Sherry, Helen, Kathy, Pattie, Donna, Sandy, Judy, Anita, Terese, Debra, Joanne, Suzanne, Angela, Anette, Bernie, Chris, and many others.

Working with people like these, and the many others I've mentioned, is really what keeps me going. Retirement, for me, still seems a long way away. The American National Bank in Chicago has a commercial on television where they feature their "small business" type customers. One ad shows a man in his 70s. The man says, in essence, everyone tells me I ought to retire, but I always thought you retired to feel good. I already feel good, he says. I feel the same way.

Recently, I've become involved as trustee for a number of trusts. I'm not acting as an accountant or auditor, but as overseer, which gives me a fresh perspective on how things look from the other side.

I feel as long as I can do the job, which I still feel really comfortable about, and as long as everybody wants me, which I sense they do, and as long as I can do it at a healthy, meaningful pace, I'm going to do just that.

CHAPTER XI
Family Comes First...and Last

Well, if it's true that you save your best for the last, that's what I've done. Ellen and my four daughters are the best. They have been and remain the center of my life.

When I was about 50, I had what I guess you could call a mid-life crisis, at least that's what one therapist called it. I said, oh, that's crazy. But I may have. I guess it was caused by a combination of just reaching that age, my father being very ill at the time and my just working too hard.

My father had stomach cancer, and I had made the tours of the hospitals with him from Anderson Clinic in Houston to the University of Michigan in Ann Arbor, where he had a pump installed that released the chemotherapy gradually. It was a nightmare for a year or two, because he got very sick shortly after I finished law school. All the pressure, I think, just caught up with me. I had accomplished and achieved so much, but somehow I hadn't stopped to smell the roses. It was a very unpleasant time for my family, and for myself. For those who haven't experienced a mid-life crisis, or whatever it was, please don't. It's no fun.

I guess the positive in it all is that I had the good common sense to realize what was important in life, and things have gotten better and better, to a point I would never have believed. A lot of friends who've had some similar experiences have asked how it happened that way for me and for us. There's no good answer to that, and it doesn't necessarily apply to everyone. But I think (1) obviously you have to work at relationships, and (2) you have to realize that life is fluid and that it changes, and people have to change with it. Ellen's been just fabulous, and I'm glad for everybody that things have worked out beyond our dreams. As I said, Ellen was a teacher after graduating from the National College of Education after two years at the University of Illinois. From everything I've heard, she was as good at that as she was at being a mother and wife.

We have four daughters ranging in age from 34 to 28. When they were ready to go to college, I said anywhere within four-and-a-half hours by car, but not Ohio State. The first condition was because I figured they'd be more likely to meet someone from around here (smart, aren't I?), although if they had gotten into Harvard or Stanford I'd have had to rethink things. No Ohio State because they always beat Wisconsin in everything when I was there, plus, I couldn't abide Woody Hayes (or Bobby Knight either). They said Woody Hayes is dead — I said I didn't care — no Ohio State. Besides, we're just a Big 10 family.

I also had come up with, and years ago passed on to my

daughters, "The Ten Truths" to live by. Although the best way to learn about life is through the experience of life, I thought it was also part of my job as a father to let them in on a few things I learned along the way.

■ ■ ■

THE TEN TRUTHS

1. Follow your instincts, even though they may not be the majority opinion. But be flexible, win the war, not the battle.

2. Everyone has "down" times. Just realize how insignificant one's every day problems are in the scheme of things and try to help someone else.

3. Work wise — do what you like to do — you'll then do it better, like it more, etc.

4. Marriage does not "solve" anything. The best marriage is when each partner has a good feeling about him or herself.

5. Daily exercise is very important — even if it's only walking.

6. Don't be envious — by any measure you're ahead of 99% of the people in the world — just play the cards you were dealt as best you can.

7. Live for today, but plan for tomorrow.

8. Money is important, particularly in times of illness or misfortune, but some of the wealthiest people we know are very unhappy and some of the less wealthy very happy. It's who you are and who you're with that really matters.

9. Helping others is often as important for one's well-being as helping oneself.

10. The four Wineberg girls are better than anyone or anything else I know — a good backhand is next.

■ ■ ■

Susan's our oldest, and she does a great job as the building manager of a major commercial property in Chicago, owned by Sam Zell's Equity Realty Trust. The way things are going, everyone in office real estate in this country will soon be working for Zell. I love his standard line, "Things are not as good as they look, and not as bad as they seem." Susan also does a fabulous job of raising two wonderful sons, Jacob and Adam. I'm sure they'll one day be proud to learn their mom was voted homecoming queen in high school.

Susan is married to Dr. Rod Humerickhouse, who is super smart and a terrific person with a Ph.D. in pharmacology as well as an M.D. They met at Indiana University and went out for awhile. They hadn't seen each other for some time after college, until she visited a friend of hers in Indianapolis and bumped into Rod. Susan came home and shortly thereafter said, Mom and Dad, I'm moving to Indianapolis, to where Rod is. I said this isn't the happiest day of my life, but I trust you, and I'm sure you know what you're doing. I just want you to promise me that if it doesn't work out, for whatever reason, you won't have any false pride and try to stick it out or do something that doesn't make sense. She said, don't worry, it'll work out. It certainly has. Rod's in his second year of a dual fellowship in oncology and pharmacology at the University of Chicago Hospitals. Ellen once said to Rod, when my time comes will you give me one of those little black pills all the doctors know about? Rod answered, is tomorrow too soon? We still laugh about that one.

My second daughter, Julie, as I mentioned, worked for both Michael Dukakis and Paul Simon. After working for Simon, Dick Phelan heard about her and asked her to be his scheduler after his successful run for Cook County Board president. Dick was one of the more famous lawyers in Chicago, probably best known for having gone to Washington as the lead attorney in the investigation of Senator Jim Wright. Wright was banished from the Senate, and Dick returned to Chicago and wound up doing a great job and cleaning up the Cook County Board as its president. Julie was the perfect scheduler because she's so organized, efficient and pleasant. She knows how to say no to people in a way that doesn't put anyone off.

I had met Dick before, and got to know him better after Julie went to work for him. He eventually asked me if I would be the campaign treasurer for his run for governor, after his four years as county board president were up. He also asked me to be his accountant. I did both.

It was a very ironic campaign because Dick ended up running against my old friend, Dawn Clark Netsch, in the Democratic primary for a chance to run against Governor Jim Edgar. I have always had great respect for Dawn, but she didn't ask me and Dick did. Deep down I guess I somehow thought Dick might have a better chance against Edgar than Dawn would. We'll never know. Dick got beaten by Dawn, and Dawn lost to Edgar.

Her loss to Edgar was to a great extent because of her somewhat progressive proposal to finance the public school system. Edgar beat up on her about it, but just recently has come out endorsing virtually the same plan she proposed. The strange world of politics.

Julie also went to Indiana University, but she spent a semester of her junior year over in England. That was the year that Indiana ended up winning the NCAA championship when Keith Smart hit a shot at the buzzer. Julie was and is a big sports fan, as are all the girls. She was in a little room in England with no television, listening to the final game on short-wave radio. They're six hours ahead of us, so I called her about 4 in the morning, her time, with about three or four minutes to go in the game, and she was sitting there with her radio that kept going in and out. I talked her through the final minutes of the game so she at least got to hear that Indiana won. I'm sure she was sad that she wasn't there because she had asked me if she could come home for it and I said no. So much for bittersweet.

Julie also married a real winner in Ricky Levitz, who was an attorney at the Kirkland & Ellis firm before joining his father and two brothers at the Greater Chicago Group, a major Northbrook insurance agency, .

Ricky is a man with many friends. Their wedding, which was quite large, could have been doubled if Ricky had his way. We told him he had to have at least a passing acquaintance with all the people he wanted to invite. Julie and Ricky have a three-year-old daughter named Hannah, and a baby boy named Matthew. They are two of the four greatest grandchildren I know.

My third daughter, Margi, went to the University of Michigan, where she did exceptionally well. It took us a long time to convince her that she wasn't really that much better than the rest of the world, but when you go to Michigan I guess that's what happens. She loved it in Ann Arbor, had a great experience and came back to Chicago and got a master's in social work at Loyola University.

She worked in the Highland Park public school system as a social worker and, as I mentioned, spent all of her summers at TWIG. For about a year, she got out of social work and joined the Phelan campaign as the staff accountant, so we worked together. She's just unbelievable with numbers and computers, and she did a terrific job filling out the campaign reports, paying everybody and keeping track of the office.

Later, she got back into the public school system in Deerfield, where she is a top-flight social worker. She has not yet found the right person to meet her high standards, but I'm sure she will. I think she ought to just keep looking until he comes along.

I have a fond memory of being in Israel with my wife and children. We were all climbing Masada. Margi doesn't like heights any more than I do, so when we were hiking up we kind of stayed close to each other and it was a very bonding experience for both of us.

My youngest daughter, Nancy, is truly very special. When she was younger she just never felt that she was a really smart person. But something happened after her first year at the University of Illinois, and from then on she had nothing but As. Quite a feat.

After working in advertising for a few years, she decided she wanted to be a realtor. She now works on the North Shore for the largest residential realtor and was voted Rookie of the Year last year. This year she's doing even better, and I'm sure she's going to have as bright a future as she wants.

Nancy is wise beyond her years. During my pre-mentioned situation she was the one who looked at me and said, what the hell are you doing? At the time I didn't have a good answer to that. She's always right up front, and I respect her for it greatly.

She was also smart enough to marry a winner. You would think somewhere your luck would run out, but mine hasn't. Scott Greenberg is another special person who is also one of the top tennis players on the North Shore — he was captain of his high school team and captain of the University of Illinois team. Scott's turned into a biker and a runner and a workout person, and he runs the family business, H. Greenberg & Sons. They have a plant in Sumter, South Carolina, which manufactures ready-made draperies, etc. He's the fourth generation, and he's doing better than anybody could imagine. He ended up getting an MBA and was also a tennis pro for awhile and then decided that the family business was right for him. I know the family is thrilled that he made that decision.

When the WHA was at its peak, I would take the girls on trips to various cities. One at a time I would take them to either Indianapolis or Minneapolis, or Winnipeg or Kansas City. We would leave that afternoon and go to dinner or go to the game and then afterwards go out with one of the players, go back to the hotel room and then leave the next morning for Chicago. I know, because they've mentioned it a lot, that those were evenings they'll always remember. I know I'll always remember them too. Although I love being with all of them at the same time, it's also been special to have plenty of one-on-one time with each of them.

I'm fond of reminding my sons-in-law that the only thing you have to do once you ask to marry one of my daughters is to promise to spend Thanksgiving with us, and be a pretty decent ping-pong player. They all come to the house on Thanksgiving, our favorite holiday of the year, and they're all good athletes and strong ping-pong players, which makes for a fierce and fun doubles tournament in our basement. I have this feeling some day they may try to freeze me out, but it's my house, and I won't allow it (actually, for estate planning purposes, it's Ellen's house), but I still won't allow it.

Ellen's brother and sister-in-law, Mickey and Reva, have been like an extra brother and sister to me, and they know how I feel about them.

I mentioned Ellen's mom helping her husband run the camp in Eagle River. Before that, she was a physical education teacher. About seven years ago she died of cancer. She was a wonderful mother-in-law. We were all at the hospital and she was in a lot of pain and could hardly talk days before she died. Her last words were to an intern who walked into the room. We hadn't heard her speak for a couple of days, and she motioned with her finger for the young man to come over. He bent down to hear her and we heard her say to him, "Son, your posture is terrible." Those were her last words.

My father-in-law Al, at 96, is a legend in his own time. There's going to be a 70th reunion for the camp soon. A thousand people may attend. If I had a penny for everyone who went to that camp and attributes a lot of their good fortune in life to what they took away from it, I'd be a very rich man. I was walking with my father-in-law and Bobby Hull downtown one day, and everybody kiddingly wondered who that fellow was walking with Al.

He's just terrific. About a month ago the lady who stays with him said that he had thrown away all the papers that he saves for me to look at over the weekend. She found them, and when he came out I said, Dad, did you throw all these papers away yesterday? He said, I sure did, Harvey. I asked, why would you do that? He said, because I felt like it. At his age, I guess you can do anything you want.

My mother is 92. We went out to dinner not long ago and she said let me pay this time. My brother and I said okay, and she looked at the check for about 10 seconds and said to the waiter, this check was added wrong. She was right. Her mind is terrific. She's still a good bridge player, too. A number of years ago we played in a duplicate tournament and didn't do very well. Afterward I said to her, Mom, we didn't do very well tonight. She looked at me and she said, Harvey, it wasn't our fault. Everybody else got better cards than we did, which is, of course, impossible in duplicate bridge.

My favorite story about my mother involves driving. We were both leaving a dinner party and I asked if she knew how to get home from there. She said she did but I told her to follow me to make sure. I told her it was just three blocks, and that I would be turning right and you're going to turn left. It was still light out so I didn't anticipate any problems. I got to the dead end and I turned right, but she also turned right. I said, oh, my, she doesn't know what she's doing. So, I drove around a big block, came back and was going to get out. Ellen said, just roll your window down and point her in the right direction because she probably just forgot the first time. So, I pointed, turned on my left turn signal and then I turned right. She turned right too, so I went all the way around the big block again, and she pulled up behind me. I got out and walked back to her car. She rolled down her window said, "Harvey, are you lost?" I came back and told Ellen, and my father-in-law and Susan, who were in the car at the time, and I've never seen them laugh harder.

After my dad died, my mother sort of came into her own. She drove everywhere, went to the theater, worked at my brothers office everyday keeping the books. Regrettably, at 90 we had to stop her from driving.

My best friend also happens to be my brother, Joel. We talk all the time. He has one of these photographic memories, and that, combined with being a huge Cub fan is a dangerous combination. He'll call me and ask what happened seven years ago today in Wrigley Field. Although I'm a Cub fan, I say I don't know and I don't care. Of course, he'll tell me anyway.

Joel got married before I did, and his wife, Lenore, is a fine woman who has a doctorate in education administration. Joel, as I mentioned, was quite a help to my dad and kept the business in good shape. He still does. Dad was also smart enough to sense Joel's potential as a businessman. It's to both of their credit how well Joel has performed in the job. The only problem I have with Joel is that he still thinks he can beat me at the card game Casino, but he has yet to prove it. He shouldn't feel bad, only Margi can.

As I said, this book is not a way of saying good-bye. It is, by way of memory, a way of saying thanks to my family, friends, colleagues and clients. No doubt, some time from now I will wake up and remember some important people I missed. I apologize in advance.

Many people have put their faith in me — as their accountant, as their financial advisor, as their friend, as their father or as their husband. It is these people who have helped mold me throughout my life, who I have learned from and loved. It is to all of them that I again say, with true sincerity, thanks for your trust.